Maria Shaw's

book of
Love

About the Author

Celebrity Astrologer to the Stars, Maria Shaw is the author of three books: *Star Gazer, Maria Shaw's Tarot Kit for Teens*, and *Maria Shaw's Book of Love*. She's the TV Guide Channel astrologer and has been in the national spotlight appearing as a love and relationship expert on Fox News, *Blind Date, Mr. Personality, Soap Talk*, NBC, and E! Entertainment Television. Maria's accurate predictions for Hollywood's top stars have amazed millions of television viewers across the country. She also writes monthly horoscope columns for national magazines, including *Soap Opera Digest, TigerBeat, Bop!*, and *Total Image*. She divides her time between Los Angeles, New Orleans' historic French Quarter, and Michigan. Married, she has two children and enjoys traveling, shopping, and Mardi Gras in New Orleans.

To Write to the Author

If you wish to contact the author or would like more information about this book, please write to the author in care of Llewellyn Worldwide and we will forward your request. Both the author and publisher appreciate hearing from you and learning of your enjoyment of this book and how it has helped you. Llewellyn Worldwide cannot guarantee that every letter written to the author can be answered, but all will be forwarded. Please write to:

Maria Shaw
℅ Llewellyn Worldwide
P.O. Box 64383, Dept. J0-7387-0545-4
St. Paul, MN 55164-0383, U.S.A.

Please enclose a self-addressed stamped envelope for reply, or $1.00 to cover costs. If outside U.S.A., enclose international postal reply coupon.

Many of Llewellyn's authors have websites with additional information and resources. For more information, please visit our website at:

http://www.llewellyn.com

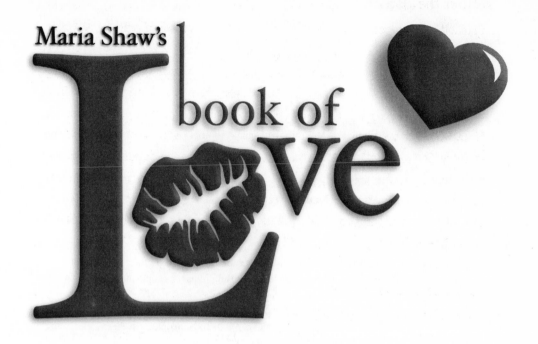

Maria Shaw's book of Love

horoscopes, palmistry, numbers, candles, gemstones & colors

Llewellyn Publications
St. Paul, Minnesota

First Edition
First Printing, 2005

Cover photograph © 2004 by Rob Melnychuk / Digital Vision
Cover design by Gavin Dayton Duffy
Interior art by Svetlana Chmakova

Library of Congress Cataloging-in-Publication Data
Pending

Llewellyn Worldwide does not participate in, endorse, or have any authority or responsibility concerning private business transactions between our authors and the public.

All mail addressed to the author is forwarded but the publisher cannot, unless specifically instructed by the author, give out an address or phone number.

Any Internet references contained in this work are current at publication time, but the publisher cannot guarantee that a specific location will continue to be maintained. Please refer to the publisher's website for links to authors' websites and other sources.

Cover model used for illustrative purposes only and may not endorse or represent the book's subject.

Llewellyn Publications
A Division of Llewellyn Worldwide, Ltd.
P.O. Box 64383, Dept. J0-7387-0545-4
St. Paul, MN 55164-0383, U.S.A.
www.llewellyn.com

Printed in the United States of America.

Dedicated to My First Love

Contents

Acknowledgments

Special thanks to everyone at Llewellyn who's worked on this project, especially my acquisitions editor Megan Atwood and publicist Jill Johanansen. Many thanks to my Los Angeles publicist Steve Allen, my website coordinator Rich Evers, and everyone who has supported me on my international tour and seminars. Also, I am grateful for the support from my family. Thanks to all my dear friends and clients around the country who enrich my life and make my work so interesting!

Introduction

Love makes the world go around! We're all looking for it. It's the thing that songs, dreams, and soap operas are made of. There's no better feeling than to be in love and have the object of your affection love you back!

For some teens, dating comes easily. You probably know a few girls who have boys falling at their feet. And there are guys who never worry about rejection when they ask a girl out. But if you fall into the same category as most teens . . . you get butterflies in your stomach and are a little afraid to take a chance at romance, then my love guide is for you!

Crushes can be fun. But if you meet someone you'd like to know better, how can you tell what he or she is really like or if you two will even get along? Before you wear your heart on your sleeve, it's a good thing to do a little digging for more info. This book can help you take what little information you already have and make better choices concerning your love life.

Let's say that you're absolutely crazy about a guy you just met but know nothing about. You may assume he thinks a certain way. It's killing you to find out if he likes you too. Why isn't he asking you out? Is he shy or just not interested? Don't make any assumptions or draw any conclusions until you read this book. You may need a little more ammunition to win his heart. All you need is to know is his birthday. It's that simple! Consider *Maria Shaw's Book of Love* your own personal love guide. It's got everything you need to help you make good bets in the game of love. Likewise, if you're already in a relationship and need to gain a better understanding of where it's headed, this book can help you with those questions as well.

Your Book of Love is divided into six cool chapters. Using a few of the most popular new age techniques, you'll find all of the answers you seek under this one cover! The first chapter is about astrology, which is based on a person's birth information. In making this section easy to understand for cosmic newcomers, we will only focus on a person's sun sign, which is based on his or her birthday. For advanced astrology students and those who want to learn more, I suggest that you seek out a professional astrologer who will use the rising and moon signs as well as other planetary positions to look at your natal chart. However, this chapter will give you a pretty good idea of an individual's basic personality and relationship needs.

Look for the compatibility guide, which lists 144 combinations of who's hot and who's not. There are suggestions on how to attract the guy or girl of your dreams, as well as ideas for a fabulous first date. Wanna know what a stubborn Taurus is really looking for in love? Would your personality clash with a freedom-loving Sagittarius? Read on for solid and in-depth love advice!

If your love is meant to be, it'll be written in the stars!

Following the astrology section, get ready to learn about creating love magic through the ancient art of candle burning. Then learn which stones and crystals to use to enhance your "love vibe." There's even a chapter on wearing certain colors to draw romance into your life. In chapter 5, get a palm reading lesson and discover what a "love line" is. By looking at the lines in someone's palm you can tell a lot about the person's love life and how he or she deals with matters of the heart. But this section takes you a step further. Just by shaking someone's hand you'll know if that person is interested in you (or if he or she is stuck up!). Take a look at your palm and see how many marriages are in your future and how many heartbreaks you're headed for!

And I've got your number when love comes to call! Numerology is the study of numbers, and by learning a few simple formulas in chapter 6, you'll know exactly when you'll be lucky in love. Is Mr. Right coming along soon? The boy or girl of your dreams could be only a heartbeat away! Perhaps you're already in a relationship and want to know if it has staying power. Love number combinations are also featured in this unique chapter that gives you honest, direct insight about the staying power of a current relationship.

Don't lend this book to anyone. Why? Because you won't get it back. Friends will want to keep it for themselves as they'll consult it a lot. Anytime you meet someone you're attracted to, look up his or her birthday along with yours. If it's a good match, you may move forward in pursuing the relationship with lots of confidence. If it doesn't look promising, don't worry. I believe anyone can make any relationship work, if he or she knows what makes the other person "tick." If you're a bossy Leo, you may have to be a little more patient with an intense Scorpio. But at least you'll be forewarned and forearmed. There'll be relationships that fall effortlessly in your lap and some that end, leaving a broken heart to heal. But there's something to learn from all relationships. Positive or negative, these are your love lessons. You have the knowledge before you now. You make the choice. Ultimately the decision of who you choose to love is yours. More often than not, your heart decides, not your head. I promise not to say, "I told you so." Have fun!

Your Love Life: It's Written in the Stars

Just how compatible are you and your latest crush? All you need to know is his or her birthday. The rest is easy. Look up your sign and then scan down the list of compatibility combinations until you come across that "special someone's" sign. In fact, you may want to read all of the signs listed so you know exactly which members of the zodiac are your very best matches. If you find that you and Prince Charming or Cinderella have a lot in common astrologically, your love life could become a beautiful fairy tale!

Read On!

After each compatibility section you will see a number of stars ranging from 1 to 5 beside the five following categories: attraction, compatibility, communication, friendship, and marriage material. Here's what the categories mean:

Attraction: The romantic chemistry between two signs/people. Do you feel an instant connection with someone or are you easily drawn to a specific person? Do you find someone cute? Adorable? Handsome?

Compatibility: How two signs will generally get along. Do you share the same interests? Feel the same way about things? Are your values similar?

Communication: How two signs respond and relate to one another verbally. Does communication flow easily between the two of you? Are you able to understand and appreciate how the other person expresses himself or herself?

Friendship: The ability for two signs to be friends and enjoy experiences without there being a romantic attraction.

Marriage Material: How likely are two signs to get married one day and have a successful marriage?

Here's what the stars mean:

♥ ♥ ♥ ♥ ♥ The BEST!

♥ ♥ ♥ ♥ Very good

♥ ♥ ♥ Good

♥ ♥ Fair, but could be better

♥ Don't bother

Aries

The Ram
March 21–April 21

Cool Crushes: Sagittarius, Leo, and Gemini

Opposite Attraction: Libra

Fast Fizzles: Capricorn and Cancer

Best Buds: Sagittarius and Aquarius

Heartbreakers: Scorpio and Virgo

Past Life Connection: Pisces

Lucky in Love Months: August and October

The Ram has the most pioneering spirit of all the sun signs. Being the first sign of the zodiac, Aries expect to be the best at everything, and that includes love! If you've got your eye on an Aries, it is most important to remember to keep the chase going. Both guys and girls born under the sign of the Ram love the chase. The harder you are to catch, the more you'll find Aries clamoring for your affections.

However, once the relationship gets too comfortable and predictable, you'll quickly slide further down the Aries' totem pole of VIPs. Some of my clients dating Aries learn quickly just how important it is not to give up their own social circle and interests.

But that doesn't always work. Aries love being the center of their steady's world. They demand it! So your best bet is to love them for their strengths, directness, optimism, and their need to succeed. It takes a strong, self-assured gal or guy to live in the Aries' shadow. If you need lots of emotional attention and constant companionship, look to another sign, but I can guarantee that you will not be bored dating a Ram. Life and love with an Aries is nothing short of an adventure!

Aries are also the biggest flirts among the zodiac signs, with Sagittarius coming in a close second. They can easily date more than one person at the same time, and frequently find themselves telling little white lies to cover up a cheatin' heart.

But when Aries truly fall in love, they fall hard and fast. They can spot people who play mind games, for they play, too! But what they really want in a long-term relationship is a strong partner. Remember, they enjoy a challenge. Their biggest challenge, however, is to compete less and cooperate more.

The Aries Guy

If a red-hot Aries guy has caught your eye, don't act too anxious! Hide your attraction, but make sure he notices you. He is the biggest flirt in all the zodiac, so there's likely to be a throng of girls goggling at him, too. You must stand out in the crowd. Your Aries guy likes a challenge as well as a good chase. If you're too easy, he'll lose interest. This is a guy who enjoys spontaneity, a bit of competition, and a girlfriend who can hold her own. If you're weepy, whiny, or indecisive, he'll lose patience. Be optimistic and ambitious. Let him put some effort into the relationship. He'll appreciate you more. Once you've captured his heart, let him know he's the best, the most adorable guy you've ever met, and everything you've ever dreamed of.

The Aries Girl

In a relationship the Aries girl not only needs to know that she's number one in your life, she needs to feel it. This assertive, no-nonsense gal admires a strong, confident guy. Even though she tends to be a bit bossy and likes to take the lead in love, she'll lose interest quickly if you give in to all of her whims. She likes a challenge and a strong, assertive guy. No wimps need apply for her affection. Do not take this lady for granted. If she feels neglected, she'll look elsewhere. She has lots of passion and craves excitement. Keep things lively and fun. And whatever you do, do not even look at another girl . . . or at least don't get caught!

Aries with Aries

This could be a decent match if you let each other take turns being the boss. The biggest problem is deciding who's in charge. These two hotheads will create the quarrels of the century, but can also turn that energy into great passion for each other. They will respect and admire each other, but their competitive nature may backfire and hurt the relationship as time goes on. Aries gals tend to be direct and to the point. Ladies, I must warn you that whatever you do, *do not* bruise an Aries guy's ego. Don't ever tell him he looks scrawny or needs to lift weights. Your Aries can easily get over an inferiority complex in the classroom. However, any jabs at his appearance or athletic abilities will surely put even the most arrogant Aries' fire out. And whatever you do, *don't* let him know how cute your ex-boyfriend is!

♥ ♥ ♥ Attraction
♥ ♥ ♥ ♥ Compatibility
♥ ♥ ♥ ♥ Communication
♥ ♥ ♥ ♥ Friendship
♥ ♥ ♥ Marriage Material

Imagine Ewan McGregor and Reese Witherspoon together!

Aries with Taurus

This could be a rewarding short-term relationship (especially for the Aries), but a long-term "thing" could spell disaster. Taureans are slow to make big commitments. They think things through. They don't move quickly and do not favor change. Taureans hold on to their money very tightly. Aries are always throwing caution to the wind, spending their dollar at the drop of a dime. They thrive on change, and the newness of life and love. Many times, Aries think before they act. Taurus' need for security may not always agree with Aries' independent attitude.

♥ ♥ Attraction

♥ Compatibility

♥ ♥ ♥ Communication

♥ ♥ ♥ ♥ Friendship

♥ Marriage Material

How about Nick Brown and Kelly Clarkson?

Aries with Gemini

Here are two quick-witted signs that love to gab. Aries love to talk about themselves. Geminis just love to talk. These are people who despise dead air. Aries and Gemini will explore similar interests: travel, movies, and a big social life. They can talk for hours on end. Even arguing can be fun! Love can grow here. This is one of the better combinations in the zodiac. Both Rams and Twins embrace change. They can't stand to be bored. These are the couples that go skydiving on their first date, white-water rafting on their second, and "anything goes" on their third! So move out of their way and watch what happens. More often than not, their relationship will blossom quickly, grow, and endure.

♥ ♥ ♥ ♥ Attraction

♥ ♥ ♥ ♥ Compatibility

♥ ♥ ♥ ♥ Communication

♥ ♥ ♥ ♥ Friendship

♥ ♥ ♥ ♥ Marriage Material

Consider Heath Ledger and Leelee Sobieski!

Aries with Cancer

The initial attraction between the Ram and the Crab is like a magnetic pull. But watch out. We're mixing fire and water here. After the first few dates, the whirlwind romance loses momentum and it's all downhill from there. Cancers want lots of attention and expect to spend all of their free time with their boyfriends or girlfriends. They need a shoulder to cry on and, most importantly, someone they can always depend on to "be there." But Aries have friends expecting them, places to go, and people to see. Cancers then feel rejected, hurt, and abandoned. Aries cannot understand the deep emotional needs of Cancers. This relationship is going to require work, and I mean hard work, if it's gong to last. On the up side, Cancers can provide a strong support system for Aries when they deal with life's little disappointments. And Aries can show these Moon children the "sunny" side of life when they get a little too crabby!

♥ ♥ ♥ ♥ Attraction
♥ Compatibility
♥ Communication
♥ ♥ Friendship
♥ Marriage Material

How about Matthew Goode and Liv Tyler?

Aries with Leo

These two signs are born leaders. The Ram and the Lion's personalities comple-ment one another. Both are confident and ambitious. There could be a bit of competition between them, but it will likely prove invigorating. They'll need to curb their extravagant spending every weekend. It's easy for a fire couple to blow their entire allowance on one night out. Aries and Leo enjoy being the center of attention and in the spotlight. These two love hanging out with friends, throwing parties, and playing practical jokes. The only challenge here is that they both want to be *number one*. If Aries and Leo can put their egos aside and allow their generous spirits to shine through, this can be a dynamite combination.

♥ ♥ ♥ ♥ Attraction
♥ ♥ ♥ ♥ ♥ Compatibility
♥ ♥ ♥ ♥ Communication
♥ ♥ ♥ ♥ ♥ Friendship
♥ ♥ ♥ ♥ Marriage Material

Ever thought about Mariah Carey and Triple H?

Aries with Virgo

Aries are too headstrong and impatient to listen to Virgos analyze their relationships. Virgos want everything perfect and will do all they can to help Aries become just that. The difference is that while Virgo is perfecting the relationship, Aries' motto is "Don't mess with a good thing." But will it ever be good enough? Aries may look at Virgo's helpful suggestions as nagging. The initial stage of romance is grand, but as time drags on, the relationship wears thin. These two are not on the same wavelength.

- ♥ ♥ Attraction
- ♥ Compatibility
- ♥ ♥ Communication
- ♥ ♥ Friendship
- ♥ Marriage Material

Would Vince Vaughn and Pink ever stand a chance?

Aries with Libra

They say opposites attract, and this certainly holds true for this fire/air combination. The Aries likes to be the boss and the Libra doesn't mind taking orders. This relationship usually works well and is considered to have long-lasting possibilities. Both teens know how to flirt—Aries in an aggressive Martian way, and Libra with a subtle Venusian style. Libras need harmony and usually give in to a fight for the sake of peace. So the Rams think they can call all the shots. Oh, how wrong they are! If Aries doesn't learn to see Libra's side once in a while, they may end up dateless on Friday night. For the most part, this couple can make it through the ups and downs all relationships experience. Remember, Aries, do not take your partner for granted. And Libra, it's okay to speak up now and then. The Aries will respect and admire you all the more for it.

♥ ♥ ♥ ♥ Attraction

♥ ♥ ♥ Compatibility

♥ ♥ ♥ ♥ Communication

♥ ♥ ♥ ♥ Friendship

♥ ♥ ♥ ♥ Marriage Material

Would Jennie Garth and Matt Damon get along?

Aries with Scorpio

One thing is for certain . . . there's no way a Scorpio is going to "allow" an Aries to flirt outrageously in his or her usual manner unless, of course, it's with the Scorpio. Aries will be deeply attracted to Scorpio's mysterious personality. It makes them curious! Rams will enjoy this chase but have regrets after the capture. They find that nothing gets past the Scorpio. There will be emotional blowups and power struggles. Scorpio will likely win. They usually do, sometimes even to their own detriment. Scorpio will push Aries to dig deep to get in touch with his or her feelings. Too much intensity could scare the Ram. The way Aries and Scorpio see life is different too, especially concerning love. I would suggest keeping this relationship strictly on a friendship level. Anything more is going to be a wild rollercoaster ride, with Scorpio in charge of the on/off switch.

♥ ♥ ♥ Attraction

♥ Compatibility

♥ Communication

♥ ♥ Friendship

♥ Marriage Material

Would Julia Stiles and Matthew McConaughey ever see eye to eye?

Aries with Sagittarius

You've met your match! This is about as close to perfect as perfect can get. Aries and Sag are bright, funny, positive, and optimistic. Here, we find a couple that are best friends, too! They can sit and talk for hours. They'll encourage one another to go after their dreams and far-reaching goals. The Ram and the Archer are opportunists who seize the moment. They respect one another for their drive and ambition. If this relationship ever grows dull, both will know when to call it quits, but can remain friends for years to come.

♥ ♥ ♥ ♥ ♥ Attraction
♥ ♥ ♥ ♥ ♥ Compatibility
♥ ♥ ♥ ♥ Communication
♥ ♥ ♥ ♥ ♥ Friendship
♥ ♥ ♥ ♥ ♥ Marriage Material

Would sparks fly between Melissa Joan Hart and Clay Aiken?

Aries with Capricorn

Capricorns play by the rules. They believe in dating the old-fashioned way: the guy should ask the girl out. Aries believe in equal rights, and breaking the rules is part of their pioneering spirit. So the Goat locks horns with the Ram. Reserved Cappy finds the Aries' spirit enticing but also intimidating. The Aries admires Capricorn's logical sense and considers him or her highly intelligent yet a bit boring. Initial attraction is strong, but may fizzle after a few dates. This combination is good for friendship, but caution is advised for anything more than just a flirtatious look.

♥ ♥ ♥ Attraction
♥ Compatibility
♥ Communication
♥ ♥ Friendship
♥ ♥ Marriage Material

Consider Keri Russell and Orlando Bloom.

Aries with Aquarius

These two have loads of fun together! There's never a dull moment. Sparks can fly when they match wits, as both signs have been called the "know it alls" of the zodiac. In love, this combination works well as long as the Ram doesn't get jealous of the Water Bearer's friends (and they do have many). Some Aquarians enjoy dabbling in astrology and reading the tarot, so the Aries needs to be open to the new age arts, or at least tolerate the Aquarius' curiosity. Neither of these signs are extreme romantics, but both are passionate about love. True friendships have been formed between Aries and Aquarius, and these friendships can last for decades. Some turn into love relationships that last a lifetime.

♥ ♥ ♥ ♥ Attraction
♥ ♥ ♥ ♥ Compatibility
♥ ♥ ♥ ♥ Communication
♥ ♥ ♥ ♥ ♥ Friendship
♥ ♥ ♥ ♥ Marriage Material

Ever thought about Sarah Jessica Parker and Ed Burns together?

Aries with Pisces

The "water" in Pisces could easily put out the "fire" in Aries. If an Aries gets really excited about something that a Pisces thinks is a waste of time, the Fish may dampen the Ram's enthusiasm by pointing out pitfalls. That's the downside of this combination. The upside is that both signs can be very romantic. They'll fall head over heels in love. However, Rams lose interest quickly and Fish hang on forever. Pisces have a tendency to put their boyfriends and girlfriends on pedestals. They'll adore you! Aries love being worshipped, but too much smothering makes Rams yawn, and they lose interest after a while and look elsewhere. I suggest a "just friends" approach from the get-go.

♥ ♥ ♥ Attraction

♥ ♥ Compatibility

♥ ♥ Communication

♥ ♥ ♥ ♥ Friendship

♥ ♥ Marriage Material

Kate Hudson and Taylor Hanson?

What an Aries Is Looking for in Love

An Aries is looking for someone who thinks he or she is "all that"—a girl or guy who will allow the Aries to take the lead but at the same time won't be a doormat. Aries crave constant excitement, so they are seeking someone who is fun, flirty, and has a sense of humor. Aries don't like possessive, bossy, or negative people. Be yourself and be ready to take a few risks if you're interested in catching a Ram. They'll push your buttons but capture your heart with their enthusiasm for love and life.

First Date Ideas

Since Aries are thrill seekers, plan a day trip to an amusement park that has the fastest and tallest roller coasters in the world! It'll give Rams bragging rights with their friends. Any type of date that includes healthy competition is fun for Rams, too. Just make sure you let them think they are the best at putt-putt golf or the fastest driver on the go-cart track. Cram lots of stuff into one date. Aries' attention span is short, so racing from one place to another may actually be a good thing. Catch an action-packed movie followed by a late afternoon rollerblading session. Grab a bite to eat and then cheer your school's basketball team on to the playoffs. Crash a friend's party or go dancing 'til curfew calls.

The Dumped Aries

A dumped Ram will rebound in no time at all. Don't mope about it. It's just their nature! If you're the one to break off the relationship, the Aries may really turn the charm on, just to see if he or she can win you back. Aries love the chase! But when it's finally over, Aries can move on to another conquest. You may feel as if he or she moved on too quickly, or think that your Ram didn't really care. Have no doubts, he or she did . . . once. But learn from the example the Aries sets; if a love affair is over, it's over. No use dwelling on the past; it's time to meet new people!

How to Attract an Aries

- Let them chase you

- Be upbeat and positive

- Flirt outrageously

- Pay them a compliment

- Don't call an Aries . . . let him or her call you

Never Ever

- Flirt with anyone else

- Boss an Aries around

- Take sides against an Aries

- Be negative

- Forget the chase

Taurus
The Bull
April 21–May 21

Cool Crushes: Cancer and Capricorn

Opposite Attraction: Scorpio

Fast Fizzles: Leo and Aquarius

Best Buds: Pisces and Gemini

Heartbreakers: Libra and Sagittarius

Past Life Connection: Aries

Lucky in Love Months: September and November

I always say earthy Taureans need only three things to make them happy: money, food, and affection—not necessarily in that order. But if your needs run along the same gamut, add loyalty and honesty, and you've probably met a soul mate.

Taurus has the reputation of being stubborn, and, let me assure you, this is not an exaggeration. Coming from someone who knows firsthand, yes, a Taurus guy can be stubborn, strong willed, and a bit lazy. But they are also handsome and huggable, and a lot of fun to hang out with.

Taureans of both sexes are looking for long-term commitment. They don't like change. That's why so many born under this sign stay in relationships that are going nowhere. Once they have a goal in mind, Taureans stick to it. So if you catch the eye of one of these Bulls, listen up! They may take their time getting around to asking you out, but don't think for a minute they're losing interest. That's just Taurus' route to love. They sit back, think about it, think some more, relax a little, think about you again, and then maybe they'll ask for your number. When you finally get a chance to accept a date, expect a well-planned evening that includes a good meal at the Bull's favorite restaurant.

Most Taureans strive for the best life has to offer. Since most Bulls are good at saving their allowance and convincing Mom they need extra cash, you'll be treated to some expensive dinner dates. You will never go hungry if you date a Taurus. But you will learn what a hot temper is. Taurus is slow to anger, but when they let loose, watch out! They are like bulls in a china store. Run for cover! The Taurus gals can be just as hot-headed as the guys if riled. They don't get mad easily, but when they do, it's usually for a good reason (or at least they think so). For instance, if you're dating a Taurus, it's a major "no-no" to date anyone else. Taurus can be jealous and quite possessive when they fall in love. They'll stick by you through thick and thin, as long as you are loyal to them. It takes *a lot* for Bulls to break off steady relationships, but when they do, it's usually for good. They won't look back.

The Taurus Guy

This down-to-earth guy is hard to catch but easy to keep. It may take him a while to ask you out, but once his mind is set on you, nothing will stop him. Nothing will stand in his way to winning your heart. He's very determined and patient. To earn his undying devotion, you must be a real lady. Make him work for a first kiss, and never smooch on the first date, no matter how cute he is! Dress up when you go out. The way to a Taurus' heart is through his eyes and his stomach. Always be neat in your appearance. Invite him over for a family meal, or treat him to a homemade batch of chocolate chip cookies. Taurus guys like to impress girls they have crushes on. Let him talk about his achievements: the winning touchdown he made last September or the math exam he aced. Since Bulls are creatures of habit, these guys like making scheduled plans. He'll assume after two dates that every Friday night you'll go out together. He wants to feel comfortable in your home and around your family, too. Expect him to be jealous of your guy friends. He sees them as competition.

The Taurus Girl

Consistency is a must in a relationship with a Taurus gal. Be on time to pick her up for a date, and always fulfill promises. Don't break dates unless you absolutely have to. Dress nicely and look your best. You don't have to be Joe Millionaire, but you should keep a part-time job, drive a decent car, and be able to afford a meal served on china every so often. Buy her chocolates and roses.

Talk about the money you're saving for the future. But hey, it's not all about the green stuff! Bulls appreciate any extra effort someone makes to please them. A little note left on her locker door will win you extra brownie points. However, like the Taurus boy, the Taurus girl can be quite possessive of her steady. (Be sure *not* to mention that your ex stopped by or that an old crush called.)

Taurus with Taurus

Both of you are affectionate and loyal. You'll probably never date two people at one time. It's just not right! In love, Taureans want and expect a relationship to last. Once they make a commitment, it's usually for good. Because Bulls are stubborn, both want to get their way, and this can lead to major power struggles, even over little things. One of the pitfalls in this relationship is that it could get a little boring, so plan lots of fun things for you to do together.

> ♥ ♥   Attraction
> ♥ ♥ ♥   Compatibility
> ♥ ♥ ♥ ♥   Communication
> ♥ ♥ ♥ ♥   Friendship
> ♥ ♥ ♥   Marriage Material

Think George Clooney and Cate Blanchett.

Taurus with Gemini

Solid, secure Bulls find fickle Twins entertaining and maybe a bit amusing. They love their quick wit and sense of humor. But Geminis may be too flighty for those Taureans who need more stability in relationships. Dating will be fun for a while, but flirty Gemini could get bored if the Bull just wants to sit home and play video games every Friday night. There are differences in how each perceives "fun," but love can grow deeper over time. It doesn't always work, but it has a better chance than other air/earth combinations.

♥ ♥ ♥ Attraction
♥ ♥ Compatibility
♥ ♥ Communication
♥ ♥ ♥ ♥ Friendship
♥ ♥ Marriage Material

How about Edwin Evers and Jewel?

Taurus with Cancer

This is a "keeper"—one of the best matches in all of the zodiac. Both are home-bodies. Both are loving, affectionate, and committed to those they love. The couple who claims they are "childhood sweethearts" are probably a Taurus and Cancer. You'll date for years, remain madly in love, and talk about marriage and kids early in life. Sound too good to be true? Ready for the bummer? Taurus can be too demanding and set in their ways for Cancers, who enjoy bossing people around. And any bit of criticism from the Bull will send the Crab off crying to mother. Cancers will remember everything you said, the date, time, and place of the offense . . . and make sure to bring it up years later, if needed. Cancers must learn not to take things too personally and understand that the Bull is never going to leave. You're stuck with him or her, but you probably like it that way.

♥ ♥ ♥ ♥ Attraction
♥ ♥ ♥ ♥ Compatibility
♥ ♥ ♥ Communication
♥ ♥ ♥ ♥ Friendship
♥ ♥ ♥ ♥ ♥ Marriage Material

How about Dwayne "The Rock" Johnson and Michelle Kwan?

Taurus with Leo

A lot of astrologers will tell you this relationship doesn't stand a chance. In my practice, I have found that many Taurus/Leo couples can make their relationship work if they put forth extra effort. It seems all of these successful relationships have one thing in common: Taurus and Leo have a lot of outside interests, separate groups of friends, and they take time to do their own thing. In general, Leos can be a little too dramatic and flashy for the down-to-earth Taurus. They'll be no strangers to heated arguments. It's a showdown between a Lion and a Bull. Everyone knows a Leo will not give up the crown. Both signs need to know they are truly loved, and if the power struggles in this relationship are too much to handle, both signs will look elsewhere for love.

- ♥ ♥ ♥   Attraction
- ♥ ♥   Compatibility
- ♥ ♥   Communication
- ♥ ♥ ♥   Friendship
- ♥   Marriage Material

Consider Lance Bass dating Jaime Presley.

Taurus with Virgo

This is a nice combination—two earth signs who appreciate one another. A budding romance usually begins with a good friendship. Sometimes these two are childhood sweethearts. Their needs are not extravagant and they enjoy each other's company. A movie and popcorn or a Saturday night at the skating rink are enough to keep the couple content.

Both enjoy eating out, and that's where they'll spend most of their money: at fast food joints. Since Taurus and Virgo are logical and practical, don't expect too many arguments to arise. These two easygoing people are like two peas in a pod. The real challenge for them is to make sure their relationship doesn't get boring.

♥ ♥ ♥ Attraction

♥ ♥ ♥ ♥ Compatibility

♥ ♥ ♥ ♥ Communication

♥ ♥ ♥ ♥ ♥ Friendship

♥ ♥ ♥ ♥ ♥ Marriage Material

Tim McGraw and Faith Hill already make beautiful music together!

Taurus with Libra

Here are two beautiful people! Both Taurus and Libra are ruled by the planet Venus, so they'll share some mutual interests. However, Venus works differently in each sign, and Libra's love of friends and "spur of the moment" parties will not go over well with Taurus' well-planned routine. The physical attraction is most definite, but for long-term commitment, there'll be problems with possessiveness on the Bull's part. Libras won't be tied down for too long. They will bend only so far, to keep the peace, then they'll leave. Taureans can be stubborn and bossy if things don't go their way. It'll take patience to keep this love alive!

♥ ♥ ♥ Attraction

♥ ♥ Compatibility

♥ ♥ Communication

♥ ♥ ♥ Friendship

♥ ♥ Marriage Material

Can you see Jason Biggs with Tiffany?

Taurus with Scorpio

A red-hot combination! You can bring out the very best in one another or the very worst! This is either an endearing, long-lasting relationship, or the craziest one you'll ever encounter. Taurus and Scorpio run hot and cold in the game of love; there are no lukewarm feelings here! It's obvious that the longer the Scorpion and Bull stay together, the more challenges they meet. In turn, their bond grows stronger and nothing can break these two apart. The key is to forget about who has the upper hand, and just go for it. Both are control freaks and have a tendency to be possessive and jealous.

♥ ♥ ♥ ♥ ♥   Attraction
♥ ♥ ♥   Compatibility
♥ ♥ ♥   Communication
♥ ♥ ♥   Friendship
♥ ♥ ♥   Marriage Material

What a pair Janet Jackson and Ethan Hawke would make!

Taurus with Sagittarius

I don't find this combination very often. You'll both have to change your ways a little to make this relationship last longer than a week. Taurus can be too bull-headed, and Sag, too blunt. An Archer won't mince words when he's mad! War could break out between them at any time. The Archer sees things from a different perspective than a Bull. Taureans want everything to stay the same. The Sag craves change and could feel suffocated and smothered here, but he or she will eventually break free if the Taurus becomes too possessive.

♥ ♥   Attraction
♥   Compatibility
♥ ♥   Communication
♥ ♥ ♥   Friendship
♥   Marriage Material

Jessica Alba meets her match with Aaron Carter?

Taurus with Capricorn

These two earth creatures can see eye to eye on most things. I'm not so sure the chemistry and excitement will last forever, but this combo is very compatible. At times, the relationship may seem dull, but I don't foresee it ending if boredom sets in. Don't get too serious about life. Learn to laugh and loosen up.

You'll discover that you're both looking for the same things out of life: a dependable relationship . . . and, one day, the white picket fence, good paying job, and 2.5 kids. But for right now, put more fun in your weekends together and take time to play!

♥ ♥ ♥ ♥ Attraction
♥ ♥ ♥ ♥ Compatibility
♥ ♥ ♥ ♥ Communication
♥ ♥ ♥ ♥ Friendship
♥ ♥ ♥ ♥ Marriage Material

Ever think Jordan Knight and Amanda Peet will date?

Taurus and Aquarius

This is a crazy combination. There'll be lots of ups and downs caused by a lack of understanding. You don't have a lot in common. Your personalities are quite different. Taureans need to possess, to feel secure, and to keep everything the same. Aquarians need change or they get bored. In the beginning of this relationship, the Taurus may go along with trying new things that Aquarius introduces, such as foreign food or new age ideas. But the longer the relationship goes on, the more strongly the Bull resists new concepts. Aquarians will find themselves fighting to keep their true identity and wondering what went wrong. The Taurus won't understand the Aquarius' quirky ways, but in order for this relationship to work, the Bull has to at least accept them if they cannot embrace them.

♥ ♥ Attraction
♥ Compatibility
♥ Communication
♥ ♥ Friendship
♥ Marriage Material

Think about Enrique Iglesias and Kelly Rowland for a moment!

Taurus with Pisces

Pisces can add a bit of magic to Taurus' world. They turn an ordinary day into a mystical journey. The practical Taureans seldom allow themselves to get caught up in fairy tales. Pisces will help Taurus experience the joy of escaping for a while through mediation, art, music, and even daydreaming. Bulls usually find Fish intriguing. This earth/water combination can do well when both learn to take the best of their signs and blend their spiritual and practical sides together. This is a very romantic couple!

♥ ♥ ♥ ♥ Attraction
♥ ♥ ♥ ♥ Compatibility
♥ ♥ ♥ Communication
♥ ♥ ♥ ♥ Friendship
♥ ♥ ♥ ♥ Marriage Material

Jamie-Lynn Sigler and Sean Astin?

Taurus with Aries

Whether or not this match will last is a coin toss. The Taurus wants to take his or her time and build a relationship from the ground up. The Aries doesn't want to wait a month for his or her first kiss. The Ram can fall head over heels in love and lose interest just as fast. The Taurus gets frustrated when the Aries gets too pushy. They won't be bribed, convinced, or shoved into anything quickly. The fires burn out fast for the Aries as he or she waits for the Taurus to light up. I would rethink this one.

♥ ♥ ♥ Attraction
♥ Compatibility
♥ ♥ ♥ Communication
♥ ♥ ♥ ♥ Friendship
♥ ♥ Marriage Material

Consider Tori Spelling and Ben Silverstone.

What a Taurus Is Looking for in Love

A Bull wants a long-term relationship with someone he or she can truly trust. Looks are important, but not as important as a good sense of humor and a positive attitude. Bulls want girlfriends or boyfriends who only have eyes for them. They despise head games and people who brag. Taurus are looking for an easygoing, down-to-earth person who believes in being exclusive.

First Date Ideas

A good restaurant! One way to a Taurus' heart is through his or her stomach, as Taureans love to eat, especially good food. So if you ask a Bull out, choose your dinner reservations carefully. If your budget doesn't call for fine dining, order his or her favorite take-out food and set up a buffet at home that's fit for royalty. Make sure to include yummy desserts. Anything made with chocolate goes over well! Slow the pace down. Don't try to cram too many things into one evening out. Enjoy simple pleasures. Maybe pack a picnic lunch and go to a park. Take a hike or a bicycle ride. Bulls enjoy music so a concert featuring their favorite band is a good pick. A long walk on the beach could end with a stop at a local ice cream stand. Order one hot fudge sundae with two spoons. But make sure that you're not really hungry because Taurus will probably gobble up his or her share and dip into your scoop, too!

The Dumped Taurus

Doesn't give up. They tend to think of people they love as their possessions. If you do the dumping, make sure you break off all communication and don't give them any false hope of getting back together. This is one zodiac sign you can't be "just friends" with, after a breakup. Taureans will hang on and hold out for years, hoping for a second chance. They are patient and have tunnel vision when it comes to the objects of their desires. Your ex will refuse to date anyone else if they're still in love with you. So make a clean break or face the consequences of a brooding bull.

How to Attract a Taurus

- Say hello first

- Always dress nicely

- Flash the Taurus a big smile

- Don't wear too much makeup or heavy cologne

- Buy him or her lunch or a special treat

Never Ever

- Push a Taurus into doing anything he or she doesn't want to do

- Cheat

- Kiss and tell

- Come on too fast

- Be inconsistent

Gemini

The Twins
May 22–June 21

Cool Crushes: Libra and Aquarius

Opposite Attraction: Sagittarius

Fast Fizzles: Virgo and Pisces

Best Buds: Aries and Cancer

Heartbreakers: Scorpio and Capricorn

Past Life Connection: Taurus

Lucky in Love Months: October and December

Dating a Gemini is like having a secret love affair. You're dating two people. My clients always laugh when I point out that Gemini is the sign of the Twin. There are two of them. I usually go on to explain the good twin/evil twin theory. The personality you see the most is a good indicator of how your relationship is panning out with this beloved sign. When happy, they talk, and I do mean *talk*. While others are walking around like zombies during first hour, Geminis are chatting away. They talk while you're trying to study. They never take a breath as you're falling asleep on the other end of the phone. I guess you could say that communication is important to Gemini in a relationship. Their attention span is short, like that of little kids. After all, they are called the "youthful sign." The twins are humanitarian, too. They love an underdog. Geminis bring home lost puppies and cheer the losing team on. There's something special about a Twin that you'll find yourself drawn to. It must be their creative side. Or is it their intellect? Who knows? But the combination of the two personalities lends itself to an interesting relationship. You should know that Gemini can be fickle in love, and anything that's dull, boring, or mundane turns them off.

The Gemini Guy

You'll need to put on your friendliest face to attract a Gemini guy. He's a flirt and a little boy who refuses to grow up. You'll never be bored, but make sure he doesn't get bored with you. Keep the relationship fun! Get creative when you plan a Saturday night out. Since these guys are always changing their minds, you need to go with the flow. Be open to trying new adventures with him. Act silly. Play together. Ignore his moodiness. Remember, he has two personalities, so you'll need to date them both! Your Gemini may have ex-girlfriends who are now "just friends." Don't demand that he give them up or you'll get the boot. Let him talk. He will talk . . . a lot. Be a good listener. Don't bring up commitment—let him do it. If he feels you're looking for "forever," he may run. If a Gemini guy thinks you're self-sufficient and don't need him, he's more likely to hang around.

The Gemini Girl

To entice a Gemini girl, a guy can't act macho, sexist, or egotistical. She's a humanitarian and believes everyone is equal. She's creative, smart, fun-loving, and can hold conversations with people of all ages. You need to be a good listener because this lady will talk your ear off! A guy needs to be pretty smart to entice her. She adores writing, and will probably send you homemade cards and long e-mails. Leave little love notes for her, too. If it's in your nature, put mushy messages on her answering machine. And if you're an animal lover, you get extra points! She adores puppies and kittens. Because Gemini are constantly changing their minds, be open to spur of the moment parties and last minute adventures. Be flexible with your schedule.

Don't pout if she's late. She's always late! The best way to win the heart of a Gemini lady is to be her best friend first, someone she can talk to about anything, and then work your way up to capturing her heart!

Gemini with Gemini

It's like living with four people! Putting two Twins together may be too much of a good thing. There will be plenty to talk about, but if no one is doing the listening, there's bound to be problems. This could still work, although personally I feel the relationship could be a little overwhelming. I suggest taking turns, working as hard as you play at the relationship, and keeping "the evil one" in check. It could be worse. You could end up with someone who doesn't communicate at all. All in all, a really cool couple!

♥♥ Attraction
♥♥♥♥ Compatibility
♥♥♥♥ Communication
♥♥♥ Friendship
♥♥ Marriage Material

Drew Carey and Anne Heche? Could they get along?

Gemini with Cancer

This is a great choice for casual dating, but anything more serious may spell trouble. Gemini will be attracted to Cancer's sentimental, nurturing side. However, both of you can be quite moody. Gemini will have to spend a lot of wasted time explaining where they've been and with whom. Insecure Crabs could make Twins feel suffocated with their neediness.

♥♥♥ Attraction
♥♥ Compatibility
♥♥ Communication
♥♥♥♥ Friendship
♥♥ Marriage Material

Consider Mark Wahlberg and Selma Blair?

Gemini with Leo

Both of you have strong, friendly, and outgoing personalities. You should have a lot of fun. There'll never be a dull moment. Gemini and Leo love a good party and being the life of it! These signs are big talkers, so good listening skills will be a key ingredient to a happy union. And Geminis need to remember not to steal the spotlight from their Leos, who need to be the center of attention!

♥ ♥ ♥ ♥ Attraction
♥ ♥ ♥ ♥ Compatibility
♥ ♥ ♥ ♥ Communication
♥ ♥ ♥ ♥ Friendship
♥ ♥ ♥ ♥ Marriage Material

What do you think of Prince and Sandra Bullock?

Gemini with Virgo

Ruled by the planet Mercury, these two are very talkative, and they may argue a lot with one another. There's an immediate attraction between Gemini and Virgo, but as time wears on, this couple will likely disagree about everything. They'll irritate each other . . . sometimes on purpose! Don't spend too much time together or the boxing gloves come out. Stay clear unless you're absolutely sure it's true love.

♥ ♥ ♥ Attraction
♥ ♥ Compatibility
♥ ♥ Communication
♥ ♥ ♥ Friendship
♥ ♥ Marriage Material

Would a relationship between Wayne Brady and Cameron Diaz make sense?

Gemini with Libra

A relationship is a piece of cake when Gemini and Libra get together. Gemini will find the Libra bright, funny, and smart. They'll appreciate their good looks, too. These two can be best buddies as well as boyfriend/girlfriend. Both like shopping, going to the movies, and chatting online. Just hanging out together can be fun, and they'll gab 'til the wee hours of the morning about friends, school, and the latest fashions. Like minds think alike, and Gemini and Libra are certainly two peas in a pod.

♥ ♥ ♥ Attraction
♥ ♥ ♥ ♥ Compatibility
♥ ♥ ♥ ♥ Communication
♥ ♥ ♥ ♥ Friendship
♥ ♥ ♥ ♥ ♥ Marriage Material

How do you feel about Angelina Jolie and Luke Perry?

Gemini with Scorpio

I'm not so sure Gemini could handle Scorpio's strong need for isolation. Scorpios hold much of their thoughts and desires deep within. They communicate through their actions rather than words. Gemini's constant need for conversation finds no outlet here. Scorpios find the Twins entertaining, but won't find the depth they are seeking in a relationship. Jealousy, on the part of the Scorpio, could be the biggest problem for this couple. Great for friends and perhaps working buddies, but for a serious love affair, save yourself time and heartache. Look elsewhere . . .

♥ Attraction
♥ Compatibility
♥ Communication
♥ ♥ ♥ Friendship
♥ Marriage Material

Would Johnny Depp and Julia Roberts be a "no-no?"

Gemini with Sagittarius

Here's an example of how opposites attract. For the most part, this could be a fun thing. These signs love travel, adventure, and personal freedom. You complement one another. However, Gemini and Sag can be fickle in love. They'll flirt with everyone at a party, but at least they'll leave together. Even though these signs possess a wandering eye, the settled Gemini and Sagittarius instinctively know they're not going to stray too far from home. You can be best buddies as well as sweethearts.

♥ ♥ ♥ ♥ Attraction
♥ ♥ ♥ ♥ Compatibility
♥ ♥ ♥ Communication
♥ ♥ ♥ Friendship
♥ ♥ ♥ ♥ Marriage Material

Noah Wyle and Christina Applegate? Just may work!

Gemini with Capricorn

Simply stated, this is the young soul versus the old soul. Capricorn is the mature sign of the zodiac. These people live by the rules and relate well to tradition. Gemini is the child in this relationship, breaking all of the rules and a few hearts along the way! These two can certainly learn a lot from one another. The Capricorn can learn to get in touch with his or her inner child and enjoy the silly side of life. The Gemini can learn how to get in touch with his or her serious side. But watch out, Capricorn, because the Gemini may find you a little too dull for his or her taste.

♥ ♥ Attraction
♥ Compatibility
♥ Communication
♥ ♥ ♥ Friendship
♥ Marriage Material

Would you ever consider Colin Farrell and Kate Moss?

Gemini with Aquarius

These two air signs are a solid combination. What fun they'll have together! They can go with the flow and are always ready to experience new adventures. They'll strive to make theirs the perfect relationship, different from any kind they've toyed with before. They can succeed. The Twins and Water Bearers know communication is very important in relationships. Plus, they're open minded individuals who can talk through any problems that arise. Gemini will adore Aquarius' quirky personality and marvel at their sense of humor. Aquarians will feel they've met a soul mate and someone who truly understands them.

♥ ♥ ♥ Attraction
♥ ♥ ♥ ♥ Compatibility
♥ ♥ ♥ ♥ Communication
♥ ♥ ♥ ♥ Friendship
♥ ♥ ♥ ♥ ♥ Marriage Material

How about Tara Lipinski and Elijah Wood?

Gemini with Pisces

If these two decide to hook up, watch out! This could be a long, drawn-out soap opera! Pisces may be too "needy" for fickle Gemini, but the Fish can keep the Twin intrigued with his or her mysterious persona for a while. Dreamy Pisces need romance and to talk about their deepest feelings. Gemini wants to analyze things. If the Fish try to smother, Gemini will run! Communications will be strained. Hurt feelings and misunderstandings arise.

♥ ♥ Attraction
♥ Compatibility
♥ Communication
♥ ♥ ♥ Friendship
♥ Marriage Material

Nicole Kidman and Shaquille O'Neal?

Gemini with Aries

Gemini will adore the way Aries playfully tease and flirt. They'll love the conversations they share, which could turn into lively debates. Aries play the role of the teacher well and are more than happy to do so. Both signs can be into mind games, so honesty and integrity should not be taken lightly. It's a safer bet than most, but caution needs to be exercised in expressing differences. Otherwise, a simple question over what movie to watch could lead to all-out war! The overall picture looks bright and promising.

    ♥ ♥ ♥ Attraction

    ♥ ♥ ♥ ♥ Compatibility

    ♥ ♥ ♥ ♥ Communication

    ♥ ♥ ♥ ♥ Friendship

    ♥ ♥ ♥ ♥ Marriage Material

Consider Ashley Olsen with Heath Ledger.

Gemini with Taurus

As long as Taurus is willing to play the games that Gemini wants to play, things go well. Gemini can teach the Bull how to have fun! But if Taurus can't get past Gemini's constant need for variety and change, they will eventually break ties. The success of this commitment comes down to acceptance. This relationship can be trying and difficult in the early dating stages, but has a long-lasting quality as times goes on.

    ♥ ♥ ♥ Attraction

    ♥ ♥ Compatibility

    ♥ ♥ ♥ Communication

    ♥ ♥ ♥ ♥ Friendship

    ♥ ♥ Marriage Material

How about Mary-Kate Olsen and Jordan Knight?

What a Gemini Is Looking for in Love

Not only do they want a fun dating partner, but Geminis want a best friend, too! You'll need to be a good listener and a smart cookie. You don't have to make the national honor society, but at least be able to carry on an intelligent conversation. Geminis want someone who will roll with the punches, not get mad if they change plans at the last minute, and someone who will accept them for who they are. They're attracted to outgoing, friendly people who aren't afraid to make the first move. If they are late for a date, don't get mad or take it personally. They're always late, so plan accordingly.

First Date Ideas

A movie, a concert, and the theater are great choices. If the circus is coming to town, get front row tickets! Geminis, no matter what age, enjoy playing like little kids. A trip to a playground or park could be fun! Perhaps the county fair is an annual favorite for the Twin. Some quiet spot where the two of you can sit and talk for hours would be perfect. If you live near a big city that has a hip downtown, hang out there for a day, grab a pizza, window shop, and catch a local band. Geminis have a variety of interests and are eager to try new things, so new places and things will likely intrigue them.

The Dumped Gemini

Dumped Geminis can move on, but their feelings toward you may flip back and forth for a while. They may even suggest staying friends, but then appear cool and aloof. They could spread a little gossip about you when they feel slighted. What is certain is that everyone will know you two have broken up. Your Gemini ex will be the first to spread the word! Those born under the sign of the Twins can move on more quickly than other signs. Expect them to be back on their feet and rebound in no time, as they can be fickle in love.

How to Attract a Gemini

- Be friendly

- Be a good listener

- Show off your smarts

- Tell him or her a good joke

- Be outgoing

Never Ever

- Forget to return the Gemini's phone call

- Be boring

- Try to pin the Gemini down

- Act possessive and smothering

- Monopolize a conversation

Cancer
The Crab
June 22–July 22

Cool Crushes: Taurus and Scorpio

Opposite Attraction: Capricorn

Fast Fizzles: Aries and Libra

Best Buds: Pisces and Virgo

Heartbreakers: Sagittarius and Leo

Past Life Connection: Gemini

Lucky in Love Months: November and January

Cancer teens are the "feelers" of the zodiac. Ruled by the ever-changing moon, Cancer moods swing back and forth. They are the most sensitive and psychic sign of the zodiac. Because of their sixth sense, they know exactly what to do and say to make their friends feel comfortable. But a lot of Cancers need to feel comfortable themselves before they come out of their shells and fall in love. Rejection is Cancer's worst fear. They can be rather bossy when they're involved with someone, but they make loyal and loving partners. Cancers enjoy travel, but home is where the heart is. They seldom move far away from their birthplace. Because of Cancer's easygoing nature, many people are surprised as to just how determined a Cancerian can be. They never do anything they don't want to do. They can't be pushed. During my many years of research, I have found that Cancer is the sign that repeatedly sees the return of old flames. It doesn't seem to matter if the relationship ended on a sour note back in fourth grade, most Cancers will meet up with their past. One problem Cancers can have is that they, too, live in the past. They have remarkable memories. They will remind you of that horrible name you called them during a heated argument in 1999, and will probably recall what outfit they were wearing, too. They save all sentimental mementos from dates and special occasions. Because they live in the past, they feverishly won't let things go. Past loves flood their imaginations. Thoughts of "what could have been" often end up driving a wedge between them and their current love. So it's important before getting involved with a moon child to make sure there are no skeletons hidden in his or her closet. If you decide to ask one out on a date, be warned: Cancer will accept nothing less than a steady commitment once they decide you are "the one" for them.

The Cancer Guy

This guy is sweet and charming. He's very emotional and sensitive, so make sure you don't hurt his feelings. He's looking for a girl who reminds him of his mother (or the type he can bring home to mom). To attract this kind of a guy, don't be too bold. Be feminine. He'll admire you if you use a gentle touch rather than a flirtatious come on. Talk about how much your family means to you. Be extra kind to his mom and get to know his friends. Do not flirt with or talk about past crushes. Even though he knows better, a Cancer wants to think he's the only one you'll ever love. He doesn't want you to have a past. Make him feel safe and secure. Tell him over and over you think he's great. He needs constant reassurance. Call when you say you will. Don't play hard to get or he'll feel rejected. When he gets moody, don't get mad or take it personally. Just tell him you think he's the greatest guy in the whole wide world.

The Cancer Girl

Old boyfriends will always attempt to come back into the Cancer gal's life. It's because she's so sweet! If you want to win her heart, act like a real gentleman. Be romantic. If you're invited to her family's home for dinner, bring her flowers and bring her mother a bouquet, too. Let her know she is the most beautiful girl you've ever dated. Cancers are romantic, and it's the little things that matter to them, like remembering her favorite song or calling just to say "hi." Even during the teen years, they're the marrying types. Let her know how important it is for you to settle down one day and have kids. When she gets moody, hold her. Don't let full moons destroy the relationship. Cancers get irrational when there's a full moon, and the littlest nuisance may upset them. Tell your Cancer girl often that you love her. Buy her mushy cards for no reason and teddy bears to decorate her room. Never, ever forget her birthday.

Cancer with Cancer

Everyone claims you two are moody, but you don't see it. That's because Cancers understand each other. You intuitively know how the other feels. Extra sensitive, you take great pains to make sure your sweetie feels loved. A relationship like this can last, but it's not the best choice. Too many emotions! Too many boxes of Kleenex! Too many full moons! However, you can lift and nurture the other's spirit during a crisis. If trust is ever broken, though, it's likely this union would not survive. Even if they agree to forgive, Cancers never forget.

♥ ♥ ♥ Attraction

♥ ♥ ♥ ♥ Compatibility

♥ ♥ ♥ ♥ Communication

♥ ♥ ♥ ♥ Friendship

♥ ♥ ♥ Marriage Material

Imagine Toby Keith and Courtney Love together!

Cancer with Leo

This relationship mixes fire and water. Although it lacks in some areas, there can be a magnetic draw between the two signs. If the shy Cancer can handle Leo's need to be in the spotlight, things go well. Crabs and Lions are romantic and loving. They both have generous hearts. However, Leos need to curb a tendency to be overbearing. It could hurt Cancer's fragile feelings. The key to a successful relationship is for the Crab to allow the Lion to *think* he or she is in charge, calling the shots in a roundabout way. Leo's heart of gold will touch Cancer deeply, but if the Crab fails to appreciate a Lion's efforts, he or she will look for someone who does.

♥ ♥ ♥ Attraction

♥ ♥ Compatibility

♥ ♥ Communication

♥ ♥ ♥ ♥ Friendship

♥ ♥ Marriage Material

Do you think Tobey McGuire and Madonna could ever be attracted to one another?

Cancer with Virgo

Water and earth signs work well together. Cancers appreciate the little things Virgo do for them, like carrying their books or buying them lunch. You both need to feel loved and adored. Give each other lots of hugs and support. However, Cancer's super sensitive feelings could get hurt when Virgo doles out advice on what to wear or suggests a new hairstyle. Cancer may misinterpret Virgo's suggestions as criticism, especially if they have to do with his or her mother, looks, or weight. If they both accept each other for who they are, then everything in this relationship will work out wonderfully!

♥ ♥ ♥ Attraction

♥ ♥ ♥ ♥ Compatibility

♥ ♥ ♥ Communication

♥ ♥ ♥ ♥ Friendship

♥ ♥ ♥ ♥ Marriage Material

Think Michelle Branch and Paul Walker.

Cancer with Libra

It's the homebody versus the socialite. Cancer will likely be left crying on the couch while Libra is out on the town. Being with a Crab means you must give him or her constant support, and Libras have all they can handle, balancing their own lives. There's lots of attraction in the beginning stages of this relationship, but it fizzles fast, as cool Libra won't understand Cancer's mood swings. Libra will work hard to keep the peace, but Cancer's ever-changing emotions stir things up. Better to be friends than sweethearts.

♥ ♥ ♥ Attraction
♥ ♥ Compatibility
♥ ♥ Communication
♥ ♥ ♥ Friendship
♥ ♥ Marriage Material

Lil' Kim and Will Smith?

Cancer with Scorpio

The emotional natures of these water signs blend easily. They may not consider one another moody or irrational as others have suggested they are. However, the Crabs and the Scorpions are both master manipulators. They manipulate in different ways. If defeated, the Crabs will back up and sidestep, using a different angle to get their way. Scorpios usually win by hypnotizing you with their eyes or sharp intellect. As long as these two are working on the same goals, this can be a great relationship! Cancer and Scorpio are very psychic creatures, but Scorpios need to share their feelings more. These signs love to smother one another. They'll want to spend every waking minute together. They're on the same wavelength. It looks good!

♥ ♥ ♥ ♥ Attraction
♥ ♥ ♥ ♥ Compatibility
♥ ♥ ♥ ♥ Communication
♥ ♥ ♥ ♥ Friendship
♥ ♥ ♥ ♥ ♥ Marriage Material

*Consider Jessica Simpson and Nick Lachey's marriage
when you think of this combination.*

Cancer with Sagittarius

Short-term, this relationship is a memorable experience! Long-term commitments, however, prove to be challenging, heartbreaking, and, at the very least, confusing. The fiery sign of Sag wants freedom. Crabs want to settle down forever. Friendly and outgoing, the Archers make the Crabs feel special but not secure. Sagittarians are noncommittal. They'll date exclusively for a week or two, then it's back to exploring what's out there in the world (and this means other relationships, too). Cancers will never understand the Sag's need to roam. Archers hate feeling smothered. These two look at love in very different ways. Sagittarius people are blunt with their feelings. They tell it like it is. And that may be too much truth for the Cancer to bear. This match produces exciting short-term love affairs because there is immense attraction. But when the Cancer gets stars in his or her eyes, things will start going downhill fast!

- ♥ ♥ ♥ Attraction
- ♥ ♥ Compatibility
- ♥ ♥ Communication
- ♥ ♥ Friendship
- ♥ ♥ Marriage Material

How about Liv Tyler and Brad Pitt?

Cancer with Capricorn

Sometimes this combination works like magic. Much depends on how deep the emotional needs of the Cancer are. Capricorn can be quite logical about their emotions. Many cannot understand their own feelings, much less their partner's. Why concentrate on abstract things? If the Cappy doesn't show his or her sensitive side, the Cancer will eventually look for romance elsewhere. What the Goats lack in emotional ability, they make up for by being loyal and protective. Physical attraction is very strong between these two. More than likely, the Crab and the Goat will miss each other desperately when they are apart, and irritate each other when together.

♥ ♥ ♥ ♥ Attraction

♥ ♥ Compatibility

♥ ♥ Communication

♥ ♥ Friendship

♥ ♥ Marriage Material

Topher Grace and Nicole Eggert?

Cancer with Aquarius

This is one of the worst signs for Cancer to be dating. Aquarians crave change more than any other sign. Their cool, aloof personalities clash with the homey, deep feelings that Cancers possess. Many Aquarius do not find much use for Kleenex, weepy old movies, and mushy declarations of love. However, Aquarians are very friendly and usually popular. They prefer hanging out with a group of people rather than enjoying a romantic dinner for two. The Water Bearer's detached nature doesn't mix with the Crab's need for emotional security and affection.

♥ Attraction

♥ Compatibility

♥ Communication

♥ ♥ Friendship

♥ Marriage Material

Brian Austin Green and Tiffani-Amber Thiessen didn't last.

Cancer with Pisces

If the guy in this relationship is strong and secure, then this will be a match made in heaven! Expect lots of happy times. If he's a wimp, there'll be problems because both of these signs can be intimidated easily. Usually the Crab and the Fish do just fine. They are both sensitive, psychic beings who truly understand one another. Romance is really important to both of them. These zodiac signs are two of the most intuitive, making Scorpio the third. The research I have done also shows there are more millionaires born under the sign of Pisces than under any other sign in the zodiac. And more self-made millionaires are born under the sign of Cancer. So, this couple could see their dreams come true in a big way!

♥ ♥ ♥ ♥   Attraction
♥ ♥ ♥ ♥   Compatibility
♥ ♥ ♥ ♥   Communication
♥ ♥ ♥ ♥   Friendship
♥ ♥ ♥ ♥ ♥   Marriage Material

What about Corey Feldman and Drew Barrymore?

Cancer with Aries

You two are drawn to one another almost immediately. The attraction is strong, but compatibility is weak. Over time, romantic feelings fade. While the Cancer is still mulling over what went wrong, the Aries is on to his or her next conquest, flirting with everyone at school. For Rams, the real excitement of a relationship is the chase. For Cancer, it's the capture. Crabs want to build foundations for the future. Aries could feel fenced in or bored. These relationships can work if the couple has lots of shared interests; otherwise, both will feel as if they're living in separate worlds.

♥ ♥ ♥   Attraction
♥ ♥   Compatibility
♥ ♥   Communication
♥ ♥   Friendship
♥ ♥   Marriage Material

Imagine David Spade and Norah Jones!

Cancer with Taurus

Cancer and Taurus fit together like a comfortable pair of jeans and a cozy old sweater. The relationship grows better with time. A Cancer will feel safe and secure when he or she dates a Taurus. Bulls actually like these clingy types. This can be a long-lasting union, one that creates memories from freshmen year to senior prom. When the going gets tough, the Crab and Bull will fight to keep their love alive. They'll stick together through the hard times and grow even stronger.

♥ ♥ ♥ ♥ Attraction
♥ ♥ ♥ ♥ Compatibility
♥ ♥ ♥ ♥ Communication
♥ ♥ ♥ ♥ Friendship
♥ ♥ ♥ ♥ ♥ Marriage Material

Will Ferrell and Tina Fey? Hey, they both love SNL.

Cancer with Gemini

If they play together, they can stay together. But more often than not, Cancer is a little too bossy for Gemini, and can seem more like an overprotective parent than a girlfriend or boyfriend. The Gemini doesn't need another mother! You'll have many fun times together, though, and laugh a lot. Geminis will help Cancers loosen up and nudge them to come out of their safe shells. Cancers will show Geminis that they have found someone to trust, to be their "twin selves" with, and, most of all, Cancers will listen. Talkative Gemini will appreciate the fact that someone is hanging on to their every word, and maybe even taking notes. For these two, love doesn't always last, but a friendship certainly can.

♥ ♥ ♥ Attraction
♥ ♥ ♥ Compatibility
♥ ♥ ♥ Communication
♥ ♥ ♥ ♥ Friendship
♥ ♥ ♥ Marriage Material

Consider for a moment Cheryl Tweedy and Chad Cole.

What a Cancer Is Looking for in Love

A Crab wants someone who is down to earth and makes him or her feel at ease. Cancers of both sexes enjoy a little romance, but are looking for permanent commitments. They expect to get married and have kids one day. They long for someone who truly loves them and will never leave them. They love it when you spend all of your free time together. Crabs look for those special connections. They truly want to discover their soul mate, and immediately know if you're the "right one." If they have their heart set on you and only you, there's no turning back!

First Date Ideas

With a Cancer, you must create memories. To a Crab, a date is the beginning of a long relationship, and it's important that the very first night out is extra special. Little things matter. Bring her a single red rose. Tell him he looks handsome as you take his hand in yours. But don't move too quickly. Set the stage for romance. Make your Cancer feel at ease. If he or she is a little shy, plan on doing most of the talking. Once Cancers feel secure, they'll start to open up and you won't be able to get a word in edgewise! A nice dinner is a good start, followed by a romantic movie. A walk on the beach is a neat idea, as Crabs feel at home near water. A scenic drive is another option, but be sure to end the date with a stop for a dessert. (Cancers love sweets!) End the evening respectfully with a walk to the door and a friendly hug. Save your kisses for a second date.

The Dumped Cancer

This is a recipe for disaster. If a Cancer truly loves you, he or she can't let go. Tears flow like an open faucet. The Cancer will hang out in his or her room and stare at your photo and old love letters. Cancers will call their psychic advisors to see when and if you'll get back together. Their outward appearance seems cool and relaxed, but underneath they're an emotional wreck! Expect a few hang-ups when you answer the phone (it's the Cancer!). In a few months, the

Cancer lets go (hopefully). There is no time limit on how long Cancers suffer after a breakup. For some it takes months to move on. For other Crabs, it's just a matter of when they meet another soul mate!

How to Attract a Cancer

- Be very polite and considerate
- Show your sensitive side
- Ask him or her for advice
- Make him or her feel at ease
- Compliment him or her

Never Ever

- Hurt a Cancer's feelings
- Criticize him or her in front of others
- Betray him or her, or lie
- Expect a Cancer to forget and let go of his or her past
- Forget his or her birthday

Leo
The Lion
July 23–August 23

Cool Crushes: Sagittarius and Aries

Opposite Attraction: Aquarius

Fast Fizzles: Taurus and Scorpio

Best Buds: Gemini and Libra

Heartbreakers: Virgo and Pisces

Past Life Connection: Cancer

Lucky in Love Months: December and February

Leos are said to have the biggest hearts among all the signs of the zodiac. Proud, daring, and confident, Leos wear their hearts on their sleeves when in love. They are generous, but if left ignored or unappreciated, they are difficult to be around. Their need to be the center of their darling's universe is undeniable. The bigger the ego, the harder they fall. That's why Leos in love are so vulnerable. They give and give and give. They do expect some things in return: undying love, praise, loyalty, and, most of all, respect. To disrespect a Leo is the ultimate sin. The way to capture a Leo's heart is to let him or her lead, make him or her feel proud, and, of course, shower the Leo with compliments. But beware, Leos know the difference between true admiration and hogwash. They enjoy being pampered, and many take great care in the appearance of their hair (the lion's mane). They expect to rule the roost with their loyal servants listening attentively to their ramblings and opinions. If their followers are indeed loyal, they will be blessed time and time again with Leo's generous spirit. Lions are fun! They like to live life large. Social status is very important to them. They're popular with members of the opposite sex, too. A Leo without love in his or her life often feels incomplete. Remember: If a Leo is happy, then everyone is happy. It's as simple as that.

The Leo Guy

He has a giving and gregarious nature. If he falls in love, he gives 110 percent in a relationship, but if this guy's efforts go unnoticed, he'll feel neglected and become a sourpuss. The way to attract a Leo man is to admire him, praise him, and tell him how wonderful he is. Listen to him talk about himself. Put him on a pedestal and let him take the lead. Leo is a very proud sign, and the Lion really cares what others think of him. His reputation is important.

Look your best. Dress well. Be charming and witty, but don't hog his spotlight. He wants the attention centered on him. Best advice? Appreciate him. When he does things for you, let him know how thankful you are. Show him lots of love and affection. You'll get it back threefold.

The Leo Girl

A Lioness wants and expects to be treated like a princess. Don't be cheap when taking her out on the town. Avoid cheesy buffet lines. Opt for at least one fine dining experience every now and then. Buy her little presents and tell her she's the most beautiful girl you've ever laid eyes on. Hint: gifts made of gold or presents that sparkle will win you extra points. She's looking for a guy who is successful and charming. You don't need to be as wealthy as Donald Trump, but she will expect you to have enough funds to pamper her. Get to know and appreciate her friends. Be supportive of her ambitions and interested in her life. She loves to be affectionate and playful. But most of all, a Lioness is strong, spirited, and generous. She can be a bit bossy. She was born with leadership traits. A Leo gal dreams big and sets her goals higher than most people. She's a drama queen and loves the attention she garners. This lady is high maintenance, but worth her weight in gold to those who appreciate her.

Leo with Leo

Major drama here! This relationship has more twists and turns than your favorite soap opera. Who'll have the leading role? Will they agree to share the spotlight or fight for it? There will be mutual admiration, and these two will make an engaging, attractive couple. It will be no problem choosing birthday gifts. Anything big, shiny, or gold will do! Problems could arise if one partner is not supportive of the other's goals. This union is sure to include temper tantrums, but heavy doses of laughter and good times, too.

♥ ♥ ♥ Attraction

♥ ♥ ♥ ♥ Compatibility

♥ ♥ ♥ ♥ Communication

♥ ♥ ♥ Friendship

♥ ♥ ♥ ♥ Marriage Material

You already know the ups and downs of J.Lo and Ben!

Leo with Virgo

Since Virgos like to be helpful and Leos love to be fussed over, this match is made in heaven! Well, sort of. Your Majesty the Lion rules, and Virgo obeys. As long as these roles are played well, love is grand. If a Virgo rebels and tries to overpower the throne, there's likely to be a royal uproar. Note to Leo: Virgo who feel like servants don't serve as well as those who feel appreciated. Note to Virgo: those who make jokes at Leo's expense will find their services no longer needed.

♥ ♥ ♥ Attraction

♥ ♥ Compatibility

♥ ♥ Communication

♥ ♥ ♥ ♥ Friendship

♥ ♥ Marriage Material

What about cute Matt LeBlanc and Shania Twain?

Leo with Libra

They both like to shop and to dress well, and they both know how to throw a great party. Leo finds Libra very charming and good-looking. Everyone knows that Libras are beautiful people, and Leos love to show off their hot dates! Lions will also appreciate Libra's peace-keeping ways. The Libra will allow the Leo to be the big cheese (a.k.a. the boss), and is happy to follow the Lion around. This couple will have lots of friends, the coolest clothes, and create the most buzz in the school hallway. Here they come, the perfect couple!

♥ ♥ ♥ ♥ Attraction
♥ ♥ ♥ ♥ Compatibility
♥ ♥ ♥ ♥ Communication
♥ ♥ ♥ ♥ Friendship
♥ ♥ ♥ ♥ ♥ Marriage Material

Consider J.Lo and Hal Sparks.

Leo with Scorpio

The handwriting is on the wall before this relationship gets off of the ground. Run! Run fast! Don't look back! But if you've already decided to try this combination out for yourself, expect major control issues. Keep a box of Kleenex nearby, or, better yet, a suit of armor. These fixed signs seldom find what they're looking for in one another. Sure, there's chemistry at first, but Scorpio will not allow anyone to truly conquer their heart or control them. The Leo will deal with these frustrations for a while, and then probably just give up.

♥ ♥ ♥ Attraction
♥ Compatibility
♥ ♥ Communication
♥ ♥ Friendship
♥ Marriage Material

Do Tom Green and Ivanka Trump stand a chance?

Leo with Sagittarius

Of the three fire signs (Aries, Leo, and Sagittarius), the Archer works best with Leo. Sag draws energy from the two other fire signs. While Aries rules the head and Leo rules the heart, Sagittarius combines the head and the heart. You won't find the power struggles between Sag and Leo like you will between the Lion and the Ram. Sagittarians will work to help Leos achieve their goals rather than compete with them. The two will love to travel, enjoy lively conversation, and can settle comfortably into a long-term commitment. Part of this is so because Sag doesn't take Leo's commands too seriously.

♥ ♥ ♥ ♥ Attraction
♥ ♥ ♥ ♥ Compatibility
♥ ♥ ♥ ♥ Communication
♥ ♥ ♥ ♥ Friendship
♥ ♥ ♥ ♥ ♥ Marriage Material

Could love blossom between Fred Durst and Gena Lee Nolin?

Leo with Capricorn

Capricorn are reserved and very mature for their age. They don't go for flashy, adventurous types, and that is how the Goat may see the Lion at first glance. Usually first dates between these two signs go nowhere and often end early. If a second date is even considered, Capricorn may catch a glimpse of Leo's loyalty and generosity. I conclude that these two would make better business partners than anything else. They both agree that career and social status is important. They just don't relate to one another well outside of that. Coming from two different perspectives, they can learn much from spending time in each other's world, but the initial attraction will likely fade.

♥ ♥ Attraction
♥ ♥ Compatibility
♥ ♥ Communication
♥ ♥ Friendship
♥ Marriage Material

Do you think Lisa Kudrow would be interested in Marilyn Manson?

Leo with Aquarius

While Leo is all about "me," Aquarius is about "we," as in, "we are the world." Aquarians could get Leos to make compromises in relationships that they never had to make before . . . thus stretching them a little beyond their comfort level. Social clubs, school activities, and mutual friends are things this couple can enjoy together. If Leo curbs the tendency to roar out orders, Aquarius will stick around. Both sides enjoy experiencing new adventures. This relationship will work well as long as both signs are open to giving one another the spotlight every now and then.

    ♥ ♥ ♥ Attraction
    ♥ ♥ ♥ Compatibility
    ♥ ♥ ♥ Communication
    ♥ ♥ ♥ ♥ Friendship
    ♥ ♥ ♥ ♥ Marriage Material

What about Hilary Swank hooking up with Joey Fatone?

Leo with Pisces

Most water/fire sign combinations don't work too well, but I find that this one works more often than not. Pisces are people pleasers. They want to make everyone happy. They have a tendency to smother those they love. Meanwhile, Leos love to be pleased. Too much adoration is never enough for the Lion. Therefore, as long as the Pisces doesn't fall into his or her famous pity-party routine or get too mushy, this combination could prove worthy, despite what traditional astrology books suggest. Both signs are romantic to the core, creative, and artistic. However, Pisces won't want to share social Leo with *all* of his friends *all* of the time. It's worth mentioning that Leo needs to be extra sensitive to Pisces' emotional nature.

♥ ♥ ♥ ♥   Attraction

♥ ♥   Compatibility

♥ ♥   Communication

♥ ♥ ♥ ♥   Friendship

♥ ♥ ♥   Marriage Material

Would Elizabeth Berkley ever date Taylor Hanson?

Leo with Aries

The no-compete clause needs to be included in the dating contract between these two. Other than that, things can work out fine. Both have the fire and excitement to excel in life. If Leo will allow Aries the spotlight every now and then, things flow more smoothly. These overachievers will be known as one of the coolest couples at school. You both have an endless amount of energy and a lot of drive and ambition. As long as you treat each other as equals, this union can last. Leos need to sit atop the throne, and Aries need to be high on their pedestals. Take turns being the "head honcho" and love will be grand.

♥ ♥ ♥ ♥ ♥   Attraction

♥ ♥ ♥ ♥   Compatibility

♥ ♥ ♥ ♥   Communication

♥ ♥ ♥ ♥   Friendship

♥ ♥ ♥ ♥   Marriage Material

Can you picture Halle Berry with Quentin Tarantino?

Leo with Taurus

A Lion may grow bored with a Bull after a month or two. When they first meet, there's no denying the physical attraction between these signs, but both like and expect to get their way. Stubborn Bulls and bossy Lions won't budge an inch if they're mad. Leo cannot force Taurus to do anything. Even a gentle nudge will be met with a defiant stomp of the Bull's hoof. So why fight? Agree to disagree, then move on to greener pastures.

- ♥ ♥ Attraction
- ♥ Compatibility
- ♥ ♥ Communication
- ♥ ♥ ♥ Friendship
- ♥ Marriage Material

How about Soleil Moon Frye and Jason Biggs together forever?

Leo with Gemini

The Twins add spark to the Lion's world. Leo's sense of humor and fun-loving spirit will have Gemini looking forward to their next date. Gemini has a way with the English language and instinctively knows what to say and when to say it. Leo loves the praise and flattery that Gemini showers on him or her, and feels appreciated. Gemini reaps the rewards of Leo's big heart. Since air fans fire, airy Gemini will support fiery Leo's dreams. Gemini can keep Leo's spirits up in times of crisis or disappointment. This is a wonderful combination, because it provides each sun sign with the ability to use its natural gifts: communication (Gemini) and generosity (Leo). Travel, friends, and the social scene are all important elements that enhance their relationship.

- ♥ ♥ ♥ Attraction
- ♥ ♥ ♥ ♥ Compatibility
- ♥ ♥ ♥ ♥ Communication
- ♥ ♥ ♥ ♥ Friendship
- ♥ ♥ ♥ ♥ ♥ Marriage Material

Could you see Madonna and Lenny Kravitz
making beautiful music together?

Leo with Cancer

This combo makes for better friends than anything else. But if you're a Lion who has fallen hard for a Crab, know that you'll have to exercise a little patience. It'll be worth the effort, because what you're looking for is what Cancer can give: undying devotion and loyalty. If you are truly ready for a long-term commitment, then consider Cancer. But if you have no intention of anything more than a date or two, move on. You'll save yourself from one big soap opera!

- ♥♥♥ Attraction
- ♥♥♥ Compatibility
- ♥♥♥ Communication
- ♥♥♥♥ Friendship
- ♥♥ Marriage Material

Would Kate Beckinsale ever accept a lunch date with Carson Daly?

What a Leo Is Looking for in Love

Leos want someone they can be proud to be seen with and show off to their friends. Leos want to be appreciated and adored. They love it when their crushes fuss over them and go out of their way to do something extra special for them. They want a boyfriend or girlfriend who brags about how cute they are and compliments them on their strength and charm. They expect loyalty and gratitude. Lions love to have fun, so they're looking for someone with a great sense of humor, a positive attitude, and a zest for life!

First Date Ideas

Throw a party and invite your Leo love interest. Lions love a good bash, and even more so if they're the guest of honor. But don't spread yourself too thin entertaining guests. Leos need to feel that they are the center of attention. They love Hollywood—the bright lights and glitz and glamour—so check out the latest movie or rent some videos. A mall date isn't a bad idea, either; Leos feel right at home there because they love to shop. Whatever you plan to do on your date, you must do it in a grand manner. Being zodiac royalty, Leos love to be pampered and adored. They expect you to spend money on them. Don't be cheap. Allow them to supersize their fries without rolling your eyes. Don't count pennies or complain how much dinner cost. That's an insult to a Leo.

The Dumped Leo

Dumped Leos can brood for a while but get back in the dating scene within weeks. Because they have a tendency to wear their hearts on their sleeves, they usually suffer some heartache. But when they meet someone else who captures their attention, Lions can rebound in no time at all! They'll fall head over heels in love and forget you ever existed. Dumped Leos will not act like they are hurt. They don't want anyone to think they feel bad. They have big egos and an image to protect. Their reputation and how they appear to their peers is important, so they may even tell everyone they dumped you first!

How to Attract a Leo

- Compliment him or her
- Look absolutely gorgeous
- Be extra friendly
- Ask a Leo for his or her opinion on something
- Let him or her take the lead

Never Ever

- Make him or her feel neglected
- Injure the Leo's pride
- Embarrass him or her
- Tell a Leo that he or she is a lousy kisser
- Talk about your last crush

Virgo
The Virgin
August 23–September 22

Cool Crushes: Scorpio, Capricorn, and Taurus

Opposite Attraction: Pisces

Fast Fizzles: Sagittarius and Gemini

Best Buds: Cancer and Libra

Heartbreakers: Aries and Aquarius

Past Life Connection: Leo

Lucky in Love Months: January and March

I often joke with my Virgo clients about how nitpicky they can be on a date. Virgo notice every detail: from the hair out of place to the ink stain on your jeans. Don't assume that you can fool an eagle-eyed Virgo. If you think you've got a zit covered, think again. Forgot to change your shirt? They'll notice right away! True, Virgos can be choosy, but they also expect perfection from themselves. They are their own worst critics. Virgos are also down-to-earth, loyal, and quite giving. Most know that their spiritual path is one of service to others, and perform their job quite well. So if you need help with homework, ask a Virgo. He or she will jump at the chance to "rescue" you. When it comes to love, there are many Virgos who hold out for years waiting for the "perfect match," thus the theory that most single, older women are Virgos. Then there's the other type of Virgo: the ones that consistently attract lost souls they try to save. Virgos are good at analyzing things, too. They have strong, quick minds, but tend to worry too much. Sometimes they drive themselves crazy by dissecting things over and over. They'll drive you crazy, too, with all of their fussing. They just can't help it. They want to make sure you're healthy and happy, and it's nice to know someone out there cares. Virgo is the most underappreciated sign of the zodiac. All of their nagging, nitpicking, and analyzing is really just how they love. They may not make their partner's life completely perfect, but they will certainly give their best while trying.

The Virgo Guy

Mr. Virgo is no doubt a perfectionist, so you need to be on your very best behavior when you're initially introduced. First impressions count, and this guy will look you twice over to make sure you are perfect! Are you intimidated yet? If you are, move on to another sign. If you like a challenge, read on! He loves brainy girls; ones that can carry on sensible conversations. He has no patience with airheads. Show him your intelligent side on the first date, your warm and bubbly personality on the second, and maybe your affectionate side on the third. But don't come on too strong. Virgos are not called the "virgins" for nothing, you know! They're not prudes, but are respectable. Other words of wisdom if you want to attract a Virgo: keep your car immaculate and your house clean. They are fussy and hate clutter and dirt. These guys love to be needed. They enjoy fixing things for you or helping out, so come up with some ways for them to be helpful.

The Virgo Girl

Like her male counterpart, the Virgo girl is particular about how her guy looks, too. She will only find certain types attractive. That doesn't mean a guy has to look like a model. He merely has to have "something special" about him. Sometimes these gals draw bad boys to them and feel the need to save these boys. Virgos appreciate boys with good taste, and those who are gentlemen and know how to treat a lady. They desperately hope that chivalry isn't dead—prove to them that it isn't by being the best, most attentive date she's ever had. Don't ever let her catch you cussing up a storm or whistling at other girls. The most important thing to remember is that little details count. Remembering her favorite pizza toppings, her dog's name, or just slipping little love notes in her locker when nobody's looking will win you points.

Virgo with Virgo

Ho Hum. Too much alike. This relationship could grow quite dull. It feels like a long date with your brother or sister. You won't find much excitement here, but there's a lot to be said for stability. Together, you could analyze life for hours, and you know exactly what the other is thinking. The problem is that there are no surprises, there is no spontaneity, and no passion! You need more "oomph" to make this last a lifetime.

♥ ♥ Attraction

♥ ♥ ♥ ♥ Compatibility

♥ ♥ ♥ ♥ Communication

♥ ♥ ♥ ♥ Friendship

♥ ♥ ♥ Marriage Material

Think Harry Connick, Jr. and LeAnn Rimes.

Virgo with Libra

First impressions go well, but Virgos may not find the stability they are seeking in this relationship. They'll have fun shopping with Libra for the latest fashions. Libra will gently push the reserved Virgo out into their lively social scene. The two can learn much from one another if they are willing to step into each other's world. This is not a match made in heaven, but sometimes it works when the partners accept each other for who they really are. Communication comes easily, as Libra intellectualize while Virgo analyze. They both enjoy good gossip, too! The Virgo will keep the Libra abreast of the latest news regarding who broke up with whom and whose parents are out of town this weekend. The important thing to remember here is to strike a balance between Libra's need to party and Virgo's need to study.

♥ ♥ Attraction
♥ ♥ Compatibility
♥ ♥ Communication
♥ ♥ ♥ Friendship
♥ ♥ Marriage Material

Consider Claudia Schiffer with Grant Hill.

Virgo with Scorpio

Scorpio's hypnotic eyes will first attract Virgo, but it's Scorpio's intriguing mind that keeps Virgo interested. Scorpios can help Virgos to loosen up, and will probably teach them a thing or two about kissing. When Scorpios go into their quiet, moody mode, Virgos may panic! They will assume something is terribly wrong with their relationship. Let the Scorpios be alone for a little while. Give them the space and isolation they so desperately need. Scorpios naturally know how to tune you out, so keep the nagging to a minimum. Learn to step back when you need to, Virgo, and this relationship could last a lifetime

♥ ♥ ♥ Attraction
♥ ♥ ♥ ♥ Compatibility
♥ ♥ ♥ Communication
♥ ♥ ♥ ♥ Friendship
♥ ♥ ♥ ♥ Marriage Material

How about Jason Priestly and Winona Ryder?
Could you see these two together?

Virgo with Sagittarius

Great friends, but the Sag probably won't stick around too long. And for good reason. It just doesn't work well. Virgos take action in precise ways. Sagittarians throw caution to the wind and forge ahead on blind faith. This couple may never see eye to eye, so romance will fizzle fast. Plus, Virgos hate being late.

They're always on time, early for school and other scheduled activities. Sag's show up when they darn well please (forget about getting a phone call if they're running a half hour behind schedule). While Sagittarians live in the moment, Virgos are steps ahead, planning for the future. This intimidates Sagittarians, who make no permanent commitments of any kind. However, count on interesting debates between them. Unfortunately, they usually turn into arguments, with the Sag bolting for the nearest exit sign.

- ♥ ♥ Attraction
- ♥ Compatibility
- ♥ ♥ Communication
- ♥ ♥ ♥ ♥ Friendship
- ♥ ♥ Marriage Material

Imagine David Arquette and Tyra Banks going steady!

Virgo with Capricorn

These two signs are easily drawn to one another. The Virgo's down-to-earth approach to life and the Capricorn's cautious nature are in harmony. Simple pleasures are enjoyed, and they both believe that honesty is the best policy in any relationship. Home, family, and good grades will be important to both. There will be mutual respect and shared interests. A quiet Friday night spent watching a movie or visiting friends will be favored over a crowded social scene. Outsiders may see this relationship as dull and boring. But to the Capricorn and the Virgo, it's perfect . . . comfortable and safe. Just the way they like it.

- ♥ ♥ ♥ ♥ Attraction
- ♥ ♥ ♥ ♥ ♥ Compatibility
- ♥ ♥ ♥ ♥ Communication
- ♥ ♥ ♥ ♥ Friendship
- ♥ ♥ ♥ ♥ ♥ Marriage Material

How you feel about Jude Law and Kate Bosworth?

Virgo with Aquarius

At first you'll find a lot to talk about and will be attracted to each other's great minds, but Aquarius has been dubbed a "know it all" sign by astrologers, and Virgos hate "big talkers." A Virgo may think a Water Bearer is all talk and no action. Aquarians are freedom lovers who have cool, quirky personalities. There's no real connection here. Virgos need to know a relationship is going to last, but Aquarians can't be tied down. Settling down is what Virgos do best. Aquarians will never settle. They are always veering off the beaten path, thus leaving a trail of dust that Virgos refuse to follow.

- ♥ ♥ Attraction
- ♥ ♥ Compatibility
- ♥ ♥ ♥ Communication
- ♥ ♥ ♥ Friendship
- ♥ ♥ Marriage Material

Would Keanu Reeves and Minnie Driver stand a chance?

Virgo with Pisces

This combination lends itself well to romance. They are opposite signs, yet both play the role of martyr very well. It's important to realize that no one really needs to be saved. Too much smothering and mothering is not good. Individual growth is a must to keep the relationship alive. Often Virgo becomes Pisces' therapist and later resents Pisces if he or she does not follow the advice given. Pisces could also become too dependent on Virgo for his or her every emotional need. The less baggage these sun signs bring into the relationship, the easier things are.

- ♥ ♥ ♥ Attraction
- ♥ ♥ ♥ Compatibility
- ♥ ♥ ♥ Communication
- ♥ ♥ ♥ ♥ Friendship
- ♥ ♥ ♥ Marriage Material

Would Salma Hayek and Julio Iglesias, Jr. have fun together?

Virgo with Aries

Since Virgos are inclined to think first and act later, they often do not agree with Aries' "throw caution to the wind" attitude. Aries is a fire sign. They act upon their natural impulses and pay the consequences later. Aries do not have time or patience to wait around for Virgos to analyze all the little idiosyncrasies of life. Initially, these two could be drawn together because of their brilliant minds, but the long haul is going to be tedious for both. A good choice for this combination would be to have an Aries as a supervisor or boss and a Virgo as the dutiful worker. But for love, rethink this one.

- ♥ ♥ Attraction
- ♥ ♥ Compatibility
- ♥ ♥ ♥ Communication
- ♥ ♥ ♥ Friendship
- ♥ ♥ Marriage Material

Consider Rose McGowan and Charlie Haas as a couple.

Virgo with Taurus

Taureans will respect Virgos and appreciate the little things they do. Virgos will delight in having a partner who is on the same wavelength. Expect many happy times together, but the Virgo may irritate the Taurus if he or she nags too much. Bulls resist any suggestions if they are being pushed or even gently nudged into doing something they don't want to do. These two earth signs can create a solid bond, and this combination is considered one of the more compatible connections in the zodiac.

- ♥ ♥ ♥ ♥ Attraction
- ♥ ♥ ♥ ♥ ♥ Compatibility
- ♥ ♥ ♥ ♥ Communication
- ♥ ♥ ♥ ♥ Friendship
- ♥ ♥ ♥ ♥ ♥ Marriage Material

What about Tevin Campbell and Amanda?

Virgo with Gemini

Both have quick wits and pleasing personalities. They will find plenty to talk about and they share a sense of humor. This combo works great for friendships, but for love, something seems to be missing. There is an undercurrent in the relationship that something is not right. Day to day, things will not flow smoothly. There is always an issue, a crisis, or something that needs to be dealt with. The Virgo may feel like everything rests on his or her shoulders, taking responsibility for all that is wrong in the relationship. Often Virgo and Gemini work at opposite ends to achieve the same means. Just be friends, Virgo. Life will be much easier that way.

♥ ♥ ♥ Attraction

♥ ♥ Compatibility

♥ ♥ ♥ ♥ Communication

♥ ♥ ♥ ♥ Friendship

♥ ♥ Marriage Material

Consider Ben Savage and Brooke Shields!

Virgo with Cancer

If Virgo can learn to curb their helpful criticism and tiptoe around sensitive Cancer emotions, things work out wonderfully. Together, these two can dream big dreams. If Cancer falls into one of his or her famous moods and clams up, Virgo can draw the Crab out of his or her shell with a dose of good humor and a big bear hug. If Virgo is in a crisis, Cancer offers a shoulder to lean on. This relationship grows even stronger with the test of time. Even if they break up, these two can remain friends for years to come.

♥ ♥ ♥ Attraction

♥ ♥ ♥ ♥ Compatibility

♥ ♥ ♥ ♥ Communication

♥ ♥ ♥ ♥ ♥ Friendship

♥ ♥ ♥ ♥ Marriage Material

What about Dweezil Zappa and Nicole Da Silva?

Virgo with Leo

There will be instant attraction between these two, but the chemistry seldom lasts. Virgo will grow tired of Leo's boastful ways. Leo will expect Virgo to follow him or her around and take orders. Virgo doesn't mind this, but needs to feel appreciated for his or her efforts. Leo can be too flashy and disorganized for the reserved Virgo, who shuns the spotlight. As long as Virgo agrees to play the role of the loyal follower and let Leo have his or her way, the relationship can last. Once Virgo gives his or her two-week notice, however, it's over for good.

♥ ♥ ♥ Attraction

♥ ♥ Compatibility

♥ ♥ ♥ ♥ Communication

♥ ♥ ♥ ♥ Friendship

♥ ♥ ♥ Marriage Material

Would Adam Sandler and Charlize Theron make a cute couple?

What a Virgo Is Looking For in Love

They need to be needed by the people they love. Virgos want someone who will accept and appreciate their help and guidance. They love making others happy. They expect you to be just as loyal, honest, and hard working as they are. If you're not perfect but a Virgo sees potential in you, then consider yourself a love candidate. If you're a "lost puppy," all the better. With their work laid out before them, Virgos are excited about helping you improve your life and fulfill your wildest dreams.

First Date Ideas

Details count and will be remembered. You don't have to go overboard with a Virgo or spend a lot of money to impress him or her, but you should show up on time, dress neatly, and have a game plan. Virgos don't like to fly by the seat of their pants. Organize the date and discuss it with them early on. They are picky about the food they eat. So, if you choose the restaurant, make sure the menu has lots of choices. Virgos are not big risk takers. A date that includes bungee jumping is not ideal. Keep things simple. You don't have to go overboard. Plan one or two activities such as attending a basketball game or a school event. How about going to a dance? A study date is good, too—order in pizza and ace your next exam.

The Dumped Virgo

Virgos who have been dumped will analyze what went wrong to bits and pieces. They'll feel bad about the parting of ways but act cool about it. Virgos can be objective and they'll rationalize why the relationship couldn't work, then they'll find fault with you and nitpick your personality to pieces. This should make them feel much better about the whole thing; they can convince themselves of your flaws and faults.

How to Attract a Virgo

- Act smart
- Ask a Virgo for his or her help with something
- Be polite and respectful
- Always be on time
- Dress neatly

Never Ever

- Nag and moan
- Lie
- Be a loud-mouthed know it all
- Act silly
- Do stupid things to attract attention

Libra

The Scales

September 23–October 23

Cool Crushes: Sagittarius and Aquarius

Opposite Attraction: Aries

Fast Fizzles: Capricorn and Cancer

Best Buds: Leo and Scorpio

Heartbreakers: Pisces and Taurus

Past Life Connection: Virgo

Lucky in Love Month: February and April

Spiritually speaking, the Libra's life purpose is to learn from relationships. Most Libras think their lives have little meaning unless they are in love. One of the Libras' biggest lessons is to learn about balance. If they put all of their energy into a relationship, they have no other social life. They miss out on the many other experiences the world has to offer them if they date the same guy or girl forever! But talk to a Libra who doesn't have a steady boyfriend or girlfriend and life is the pits! It's like Christmas without presents! Libras are ruled by the planet Venus, and are undoubtedly some of the most attractive people. They have strong creative natures and make excellent artists, writers, and musicians. Many Libras enter the law field when they get older, as they believe strongly in justice for all. If a friend is being mistreated, it's usually a Libra who speaks up to defend the victim.

In love, Libras tend to bend over backward to keep peace and harmony. They hate confrontation. They will avoid it at any cost, even to their own detriment. Libras have high standards in love. They are always searching for that "perfect person," the one they've dreamed about since first grade. Seldom do they meet someone who can fit the bill, so Libras need to bring their unrealistic view of love down a notch in order to be satisfied. If they refuse, they will surely be disappointed time and time again. Once committed, the social Libra still likes to party, so it's important for them to choose a partner who isn't jealous when they hang out with their friends.

The Libra Guy

Libra guys have a grand idea of what their dream girl is supposed to look like. In reality, no one is likely to match their ideals, but if you have your heart set on a Libra, go ahead and give it your best shot. Always look dynamite when you see him. Be charming. Don't be afraid to take the lead in the relationship, because sometimes this guy prefers that you do. He plays fair and doesn't appreciate chaos in his life. He expects his world to be peaceful and harmonious. Understand that he'll change his mind about serious commitment many times. Practice patience. It will pay off, and he'll be the most romantic date you'll ever have. He's a real cutie. The only problem is . . . he knows it!

The Libra Girl

She loves romance. In fact, to a Libra lady, love is what life is all about. Be attentive and caring. Indulge her with cute little gifts and keepsakes. She is quite the social butterfly, fluttering around, charming everyone, so make sure she notices you. Compliment her on her cute outfit or her pretty hair. Bring her pink roses and candy. Never swear or lose your temper. Libras hate vulgarity. Friendships are important to her, so be extra nice to those she cares about. She is likely to be very pretty, but don't let that intimidate you. She appreciates a strong, self-assured guy who can be her knight in shining armor. Remember, romance is what she lives for!

Libra with Libra

Two Libras make a beautiful couple. However, they are inclined to party or socialize too much when they're together. Watch out for falling grades and upset parents! Too much of a good thing may not be so good. But these two love being in love. You'll see them walking hand-in-hand in the hall, attached at the hip, acting all goofy and love struck. The world revolves around them . . . they think. They've found their soul mate—at least for now.

♥ ♥ ♥ ♥ Attraction

♥ ♥ ♥ Compatibility

♥ ♥ ♥ ♥ ♥ Communication

♥ ♥ ♥ ♥ Friendship

♥ ♥ ♥ ♥ Marriage Material

Think of Tommy Lee and Catherine Zeta-Jones.

Libra with Scorpio

Libra will be drawn to Scorpio almost immediately. Scorpio will shower Libra with lots of attention, but may be jealous of friends who want to monopolize all of Libra's time. Libra will find Scorpio intensely passionate, but also a bit controlling. Social Libra may feel as if he or she is the one always bending to keep the peace. This can work as long Libra agrees to give in to Scorpio's demands.

♥ ♥ ♥ Attraction

♥ ♥ Compatibility

♥ ♥ Communication

♥ ♥ ♥ Friendship

♥ ♥ Marriage Material

Snoop Dogg and Brittany Murphy?

Libra with Sagittarius

Libras are looking for a steady commitment with someone who is outgoing and a lot of fun. Sagittarians fit that bill, except they're looking for something a little less permanent. This combination still holds promise. If the Sag teen is mature, then Libra is a good choice for dating. The Archer will adore everything about Libra—his or her wit, charm, and warm personality. The match makes for a great friendship, too!

♥ ♥ ♥ ♥ Attraction
♥ ♥ ♥ ♥ Compatibility
♥ ♥ ♥ Communication
♥ ♥ ♥ ♥ ♥ Friendship
♥ ♥ ♥ ♥ Marriage Material

Would Usher get along with Lucy Liu?

Libra with Capricorn

You've got your work cut out for you if you're the Libra in this relationship! Cappy likes the way Libra looks and dresses, but may feel Libra has his or her "head in the clouds." Libra may feel Capricorn is a little to "blah" for his or her taste. Although they'll admire one another for their personal style and good looks, there's not enough depth to keep both of them interested for long.

♥ ♥ ♥ Attraction
♥ ♥ Compatibility
♥ Communication
♥ ♥ Friendship
♥ Marriage Material

Consider Simon Cowell and Belinda Chapple!

Libra with Aquarius

Libra and Aquarius both understand the need for change and personal space. These two air signs have much in common: lots of friends, a strong creative side, and a love of animals. Both are humanitarians at heart. Sometimes Aquarius can be a little too cool and aloof for Libra's romantic side. The Water Bearer is not one to whisper sweet nothings into thin air. But Libra can help draw Aquarius' deeply buried sensitive side to the surface.

♥ ♥ ♥ ♥   Attraction
♥ ♥ ♥ ♥   Compatibility
♥ ♥ ♥ ♥   Communication
♥ ♥ ♥ ♥   Friendship
♥ ♥ ♥ ♥ ♥   Marriage Material

Do you ever think Avril Lavigne and Vince Carter could be a couple?

Libra with Pisces

Romance is high on both of your lists. You love to be in love, but long-term compatibility is another story. Libras adore the dreamy Pisces. The relationship seems like a romance novel filled with Pisces' flowery words and kisses. When the last chapter is read, reality sets in. Pisces may be too smothering and suffocating for social butterflies like Libra. This couple can dream big, beautiful dreams together, but rarely are those dreams fulfilled.

♥ ♥ ♥   Attraction
♥ ♥   Compatibility
♥ ♥ ♥   Communication
♥ ♥   Friendship
♥ ♥   Marriage Material

Seann William Scott on a date with Kirsten Davis?

Libra with Aries

Libra is willing to let Aries lead. That's one of the main reasons this match has staying power. These two genuinely like each other. Libra doesn't mind if Aries flirts with everybody in town because Libra is too busy doing the same! It's usually harmless fun. Libra can twist even the strongest Aries around his or her little finger. That's because Libras have a tendency to put their partners on pedestals and Aries believe they belong there. Libra's undying devotion gives Aries the reassurance he or she needs that this relationship is truly special. Aries, in turn, showers Libra with his or her own brand of love and affection.

70

♥ ♥ ♥ ♥ Attraction
♥ ♥ ♥ Compatibility
♥ ♥ Communication
♥ ♥ ♥ Friendship
♥ ♥ ♥ ♥ Marriage Material

Do you ever see Jenna Elfman hooking up with Tommy Haas?

Libra with Taurus

Both ruled by the planet Venus, Libra and Taurus will enjoy many of the same luxuries in life: good food, music, art, and nice clothes. Taurus, however, will not agree with the way shopaholic Libra spends his or her money. Libra thinks Taurus is a tightwad. Taureans have some of the same likes, but their personality types may clash. Taurus will be jealous of the time Libra spends with friends. The possessive Taurean nature may be too much for Libra to handle. At some point, Libra will ask, "What's more important: a good dinner date or personal freedom?"

♥ ♥ ♥ Attraction
♥ ♥ Compatibility
♥ ♥ Communication
♥ ♥ ♥ Friendship
♥ ♥ Marriage Material

Is Dylan Neal even a remote possibility with Sarah Hughes?

Libra with Gemini

Creative Libra and Gemini often meet for the first time in an art or music class. If not, it's most likely at a mutual friend's party, as both are social butterflies. They love to have fun! They'll always be little kids at heart, and often look younger than their ages reveal. These air signs will gab for hours on the phone and still find it hard to hang up and say goodnight. This could be the very relationship you've been waiting for!

♥ ♥ ♥ ♥ Attraction
♥ ♥ ♥ ♥ Compatibility
♥ ♥ ♥ ♥ ♥ Communication
♥ ♥ ♥ ♥ Friendship
♥ ♥ ♥ ♥ ♥ Marriage Material

What do you have to say about Nicky Hilton and Maxwell going out?

Libra with Cancer

The easygoing natures of both signs are a plus, but shy Cancer may turn out to be a drag for outgoing Libra, who wants to attend every party and social event of the season. Sure, there's lots of chemistry here, and Libra will think that Cancer is oh, so sweet, but the initial attraction that brought these two together will likely wane. Misunderstandings leave Libra running to cry on his or her friend's shoulder and Cancer retreating into his or her safe shell.

♥ ♥ ♥ Attraction
♥ ♥ Compatibility
♥ ♥ Communication
♥ ♥ ♥ Friendship
♥ ♥ Marriage Material

Simon Cowell and Lil' Kim would never make a love match!

Libra with Leo

This combination works better if the guy here is a Leo because the Libra lady will have someone to admire and put on a pedestal. Plus, her friends will think he's so cool! But if the guy's a Libra, this couple will still have lots of fun. There will be parties, mutual friends, homecoming dances, and great big hugs. However, a Leo gal may prefer a more aggressive partner to match her smarts.

♥ ♥ ♥ ♥　Attraction
♥ ♥ ♥ ♥　Compatibility
♥ ♥ ♥ ♥　Communication
♥ ♥ ♥ ♥ ♥　Friendship
♥ ♥ ♥ ♥　Marriage Material

Gwyneth Paltrow with Christian Slater? Now that's interesting!

Libra with Virgo

Libra likes the fact that Virgo has all the answers! Virgos are very smart. That's great if you need a study partner. However, ask a Libra how a Friday night date went, and he or she will answer in one word: "Boring!" Plus, Libra's indecisive nature will drive Virgo up the wall. Time is valuable to Virgo and should not be wasted. These two signs have great minds, but it is their values that may differ. Libras will not sweat the small stuff. They look at the big picture. Virgos, on the other hand, scrutinize every detail. They must have all angles covered before they step out into traffic.

♥ ♥　Attraction
♥ ♥　Compatibility
♥ ♥　Communication
♥ ♥ ♥ ♥　Friendship
♥ ♥　Marriage Material

Consider Neve Campbell and Jimmy Fallon?

What a Libra Is Looking for in Love

A Libra wants someone who is romantic to the core—a guy or girl who is attractive, bold, and never allows a date to get boring. They want you to call them all the time, be by their side, and adore their friends. You can't hassle them about spending too much time with their best buds or for showing up late. Libras love people with easygoing, laid back personalities. They don't want to fight with you, but if they do, Libras will be the first to kiss and make up.

First Date Ideas

Dress up and go where the people are! Your first date may be best if you include another couple. A double date would make everyone feel comfortable, and there'd be plenty to talk about if the conversation lags. Give your Libra a reason to dress up and pamper himself or herself. Expect him or her to be a little late, as Libras need extra time to get ready. Set the mood by playing your Libra's favorite CD. Plan on ordering appetizers instead of a big dinner, as Libras usually don't eat a lot at one time. You can always stop for a snack later.

The Dumped Libra

The dumped Libra will cry and pout for a week or so, then let everyone know that he or she is back on the market. It doesn't take long for Libra to find someone new after he or she has broken off a relationship. Libras hate to be alone. In fact, they probably had someone else already lined up to ask out when things turned sour with you. Don't worry about dumped Libras, they'll land on their feet every time!

How to Attract a Libra

- Flirt in a friendly way
- Dress attractively
- Be romantic
- Be able to hold a conversation
- Have a positive attitude

Never Ever

- Swear in a Libra's presence
- Treat people rudely
- Make disgusting noises
- Create a scene
- Develop a bad reputation

Scorpio
The Scorpion
October 24–November 22

Cool Crushes: Capricorn and Pisces

Opposite Attraction: Taurus

Fast Fizzles: Leo and Aquarius

Best Buds: Cancer and Virgo

Heartbreakers: Aries and Sagittarius

Past Life Connection: Libra

Lucky in Love Months: March and May

A relationship with a Scorpio will change your life forever. You'd never guess just how strong-willed and determined they really are because they seem so laid back and easygoing, and maybe even a little bit shy. That's what they want you to think. They're just sizing you up. Scorpios have poker faces that don't give away their true feelings—but their eyes do. If you happen across a pair of penetrating hypnotic eyes, the ones that draw you from across a room, there's a Scorpio in your midst. Seldom do they let any emotion show unless they are extremely angry. Scorpios are very controlled. They like to control their relationships, too. It makes them feel safe.

They trust no one, as they are suspicious creatures, so you must earn a Scorpio's trust. Once you do, you will have a loyal comrade forever. Scorpios are hard to get to know, but it will be worth making the effort. They are the best at mind games and are known to be master manipulators. They usually end up getting their way, one way or another. Scorpios have gained a sexy reputation. They are known to be the best kissers among the sun signs.

In love, they are intense, deeply wounded when hurt, and can be revengeful, but when they completely open their hearts and learn to trust, a relationship with a Scorpio can be an intense spiritual experience like no other. The Scorpio will sense your needs, touch your heart, and then capture your soul.

The Scorpio Guy

This guy appears laid back and easygoing, and it seems as if he wouldn't hurt a fly. But guess again. Beneath his cool, calm exterior lies a deep intensity and passion that can't be matched by any other sign in the zodiac. You need to earn his trust. Consistency is the key. The Scorpio guy likes girls who are down-to-earth and a little bit of a challenge. He is intuitive, so don't lie or manipulate him. He'll catch on right away. Be considerate of his feelings, but don't allow him to walk all over yours. His moodiness could drive you a little mad but his other qualities will make up that. Don't attempt to make him jealous. He is paranoid as it is, and smells evil when it doesn't exist. Plus, he'll feel you're untrustworthy. He likes to feel safe and in control in a relationship. After time, your Scorpio guy will be loyal, caring, and devoted to you and only you (as long as he thinks he's getting his way).

The Scorpio Girl

If you want to get to know a Scorpio girl, practice patience and perseverance. She, like her male counterpart, needs to trust you completely before she commits. Make sure you are up for the challenge, because this lady is like no one you have ever met before. Be honest. She'll know if you're lying. Be attentive and on time. If you make a promise, keep it. Scorpios don't forget. She is sensitive, but doesn't always show it. Her poker face will never reveal if she's really interested in you. But once you win her heart, you'll know for sure where this intense girl stands. She's jealous of any other girl that looks your way. Once she feels safe with you, she will be extremely loyal and affectionate. She needs to have control at all times, but she loses interest in wimps, so one must walk a fine line between being a doormat and a really cool guy.

Scorpio with Scorpio

These are two intense, magnetic personalities, and both want to control their own destiny. As a Scorpio, you're not intimidated by anything or anyone, but you could be intimidated by each other. You're intrigued by members of your own sign. Can you make a relationship last? There will be control issues to contend with, and some knock-'em-down, drag-'em-out fights. Let's hope these two don't use voodoo dolls when they're angry! One of the nicest things I can say is that you as a Scorpio will finally have found someone who truly understands you.

 ♥ ♥ ♥ Attraction
 ♥ ♥ ♥ Compatibility
 ♥ ♥ ♥ ♥ Communication
 ♥ ♥ ♥ ♥ Friendship
 ♥ ♥ ♥ ♥ Marriage Material

Think of Leonardo DiCaprio and Tara Reid.

Scorpio with Sagittarius

A few casual dates may be all that comes of this match-up. Sag wants freedom while Scorpio wants commitment. The early stages of romance are wonderful, but the momentum will eventually dwindle. This is not a relationship Sagittarians could easily pop in and out of, like they do with other signs. Scorpios want all or nothing. You've been properly warned, Sag!

 ♥ ♥ ♥ Attraction
 ♥ ♥ Compatibility
 ♥ ♥ Communication
 ♥ ♥ ♥ ♥ Friendship
 ♥ Marriage Material

What about Sisqo along with Jenna Bush?

Scorpio with Capricorn

Here we find that physical attraction is strong, and Scorpio feels safe with Capricorn. These two will argue back and forth because Capricorn is very opinionated and Scorpio likes to have the upper hand. Surprisingly, these two can kiss and make up more quickly after an argument than any of the other signs (even though Scorpios can hold grudges). This has all of the makings of a long-term love affair.

♥ ♥ ♥ ♥ Attraction
♥ ♥ ♥ ♥ Compatibility
♥ ♥ ♥ Communication
♥ ♥ ♥ ♥ Friendship
♥ ♥ ♥ ♥ Marriage Material

Would Lauren Ambrose date Ricky Martin?

Scorpio with Aquarius

These two can really get on each other's nerves over the silliest little things. The independent Aquarius nature is too much for a Scorpio to handle. Plus, a Water Bearer's cool attitude doesn't fill the sensitive Scorpio's emotional needs. Scorpios will never hear the declarations of love they desire. The only way for this relationship to make it past a month is if it were a long-distance one. It's going to be difficult. I'd avoid going down this road.

♥ ♥ Attraction
♥ Compatibility
♥ Communication
♥ ♥ Friendship
♥ Marriage Material

You know two people who have tried this before . . .
Demi Moore and Ashton Kutcher!

Scorpio with Pisces

These two water signs complement each other. Pisces is very helpful and caring, and in turn, Scorpios are loyal and supportive. Both signs are like sponges. They tend to soak up other people's problems and feelings, so you will understand one another very well! Pisces also smother their loved ones, and that should make Scorpios feel very loved and secure. However, Scorpios have a deep need for intervals of isolation. They could resent Pisces crowding their space. If the Pisces guy or girl has a strong personality, this pair can weave magic into their everyday lives.

♥ ♥ ♥ ♥ Attraction
♥ ♥ ♥ ♥ Compatibility
♥ ♥ ♥ ♥ Communication
♥ ♥ ♥ ♥ ♥ Friendship
♥ ♥ ♥ ♥ ♥ Marriage Material

If Nick Lachey were single would he consider asking Charlotte Church out?

Scorpio with Aries

You're mixing fire and water when these two signs get together. Most Scorpios can see right through Aries' mind games and power plays. At times, sparks will fly between them, but the attraction seldom lasts. Both want to be in the driver's seat. These relationships will be a real challenge. Jealous Scorpio will not stand for Aries' wandering eye. The time and energy spent on trying to make this relationship work is not worth the end result. Both try to manipulate to gain the upper hand. Trust, or the lack of it, will be a big problem.

♥ ♥ Attraction
♥ Compatibility
♥ Communication
♥ ♥ Friendship
♥ Marriage Material

Can you see Kelly Osbourne with Jason Kidd?

Scorpio with Taurus

"I've met my match," cries the delighted Scorpio. Taurus' energy and drive is almost as strong as Scorpio's. These two hard-headed, jealous, possessive signs will bring out the best in one another . . . and the worst! Expect loyalty, true love, and admiration. If you're both working toward the same goals and not against one another, you can be a dynamite couple!

♥ ♥ ♥ ♥ Attraction
♥ ♥ ♥ ♥ Compatibility
♥ ♥ ♥ Communication
♥ ♥ ♥ ♥ Friendship
♥ ♥ ♥ ♥ Marriage Material

Is Kirsten Dunst compatible with P. Diddy?

Scorpio with Cancer

These emotional, psychic signs know just the right thing to say or do to lift each other's spirits. If they are both depressed at the same time, we have quite a problem! They love being together and can't stand being apart. Scorpio and Cancer have photographic minds. They don't miss anything. It's important that they fight fair and agree to peace treaties. Both are excellent at manipulating situations to their benefit. Scorpios have to make sure that their stinging criticisms don't hurt the Crabs. Cancers need to learn not to take things too personally.

♥ ♥ ♥ ♥ Attraction
♥ ♥ ♥ ♥ ♥ Compatibility
♥ ♥ ♥ ♥ Communication
♥ ♥ ♥ ♥ Friendship
♥ ♥ ♥ ♥ ♥ Marriage Material

I could see Heather Tom and Tom Cruise on a date!

Scorpio with Leo

Scorpios won't ride on the passenger side. They want to be in the driver's seat in their relationships. This ride won't last long with Leo the Lion. Domineering Leo will want Scorpio to be a faithful and loyal servant. Royal Leo roars, "I am your leader." Scorpio bows to no one. Expect heated exchanges and major power struggles. Leo may think he or she is winning this battle, but Scorpio will ultimately win the war, even if it means the death of the relationship.

- ♥ ♥ Attraction
- ♥ Compatibility
- ♥ ♥ Communication
- ♥ ♥ Friendship
- ♥ Marriage Material

Do you think Lauren Ambrose would ever notice Donnie Wahlberg?

Scorpio with Virgo

What begins as a close friendship may lead to something more! Scorpio and Virgo can make that transition easily. Arguments are likely to be over little silly things that don't seem so silly at the time. Scorpio will resort to the silent-treatment tactic, and Virgo will try to analyze the root of the problem. The best antidote for a happier love life between the two is not to sweat the small stuff. Most of the time this combination works great, but Virgo must accept the fact that being in love with any Scorpio is never easy.

- ♥ ♥ ♥ ♥ Attraction
- ♥ ♥ ♥ ♥ Compatibility
- ♥ ♥ ♥ Communication
- ♥ ♥ ♥ ♥ Friendship
- ♥ ♥ ♥ ♥ Marriage Material

What about Winona Ryder and Jonathan Taylor Thomas?

Scorpio with Libra

There's mutual admiration and attraction, but the fireworks don't last. Scorpio isn't going to find the depth and intensity he or she seeks in a relationship here; there is not enough drama. Scorpios are not afraid of confrontation. They enjoy a good battle. Libras run from battle. It takes two to fight. Sometimes when things run smoothly in a relationship, Scorpios will try to stir the pot a little, to cause some friction. The relationship seems more exciting to them that way. More importantly, they'll get the chance to kiss and make up! Peace-loving Libra won't be a part of this soap opera for long!

♥ ♥ ♥ Attraction

♥ ♥ Compatibility

♥ ♥ Communication

♥ ♥ ♥ ♥ Friendship

♥ ♥ Marriage Material

Would Rebecca Romijn like Kurt Thomas?

What a Scorpio Is Looking for in Love

Scorpios are seeking a very deep, intense connection. They believe in soul mates and are very passionate when they fall in love. They long for someone who can understand the depth of their emotions and insecurities, as well as their need for isolation at times. They are great judges of character and aren't impressed with braggers and boastful people who long to be the center of attention. They want a loyal, dedicated partner who's just as affectionate as they are.

First Date Ideas

A murder mystery dinner or scary movie with a great plot would make an excellent choice. Or maybe a romantic stroll in the moonlight or window shopping downtown after the stores are all closed. Scorpios are night creatures. Hang out and stay up late. Go see a psychic and get your tarot cards read. Scorpios want to avoid the crowds. They love to spend quiet moments with the people they love.

The Dumped Scorpio

If you want to make a clean break from your Scorpio, better let your Scorpio think it was his or her idea. Back away from the relationship slowly. If Scorpios get hurt, they may seek revenge! Not all do, but it'll cross their minds. If they truly want you back, they will stop at nothing to win your heart again. They will use whatever manipulation tactics they can. Be absolutely sure you want to break up with a Scorpio, because when they are truly over someone, Scorpios will close the door to their hearts to that person . . . and seal it forever.

How to Attract a Scorpio

- Be mysterious

- Tell him or her you have a secret

- Throw subtle come-ons his or her way

- Read a Scorpio's palm

- Ask him or her to help you solve a problem

Never Ever

- Date a Scorpio's best friend

- Criticize his or her ideas

- Ask too many personal questions

- Give a Scorpio an ultimatum

- Lie or cheat

Sagittarius
The Archer
November 23–December 22

Cool Crushes: Aries, Leo, and Aquarius

Opposite Attraction: Gemini

Fast Fizzles: Cancer, Virgo, and Pisces

Best Buds: Scorpio and Aquarius

Heartbreakers: Cancer and Pisces

Past Life Connection: Scorpio

Lucky in Love Months: June and October

These are the Don Juans of the zodiac. The Sagittarius guys and gals are some of the most charming people you'll ever come into contact with. Sagittarius girls are more thoughtful, however, when it comes to breaking off relationships than guys are. Most Sag guys think nothing of dating several girls at the same time. They are notoriously known for their little black books.

The guys can be immature, but that doesn't matter to those girls that fall madly in love with them. They know how to dish out the compliments and make their girlfriends feel as if they are truly princesses. Their fear is settling down. A Sagittarius guy will stay single as long as he can.

The Sagittarius gal is strong, poised, and brutally honest. She will be a counselor to all of her friends, yet she hates to burden others with her own troubles. She is optimistic and happy. People love to be around her. She is looking for a boyfriend who can also be her best friend.

Communication is a must in any relationship with Sag. Many Archers prefer dating people a year or two younger than they are. Most of their friends are secretly in love with them!

Sagittarians are lucky people. They seem to get out of sticky situations with ease and have an extra guardian angel hovering over their shoulders.

When they do settle down, they never settle. They make sure their partners will give them the encouragement they need and the freedom to be themselves.

Even after they choose to date someone seriously, some Archers keep their romantic options open.

They make excellent athletes or members of the school's debate team. They can't wait until they get their first set of wheels. To love a Sagittarius is an adventure like no other. You must have a strong heart and an open mind. Be ready to let the good times roll!

The Sagittarius Guy

This guy makes you feel truly special when you're with him. But be forewarned, he could be smiling at another girl when you excuse yourself to powder your nose. Understand that no one will ever tie him down. The way to catch these career bachelors is to first and foremost be their best friend. Join in on the activities he prefers to do. Don't ever talk about commitment or the future. Let him bring it up, and when he does, don't act overanxious. Keep your relationship interesting. If you fall into a rut, the Sagittarius guy will look for greener pastures. Try to always be upbeat, positive, and ready to change your schedule at the last minute, without complaining. Sag guys hate naggers. They don't want to feel fenced in. They prefer girls who are independent, can roll with the punches, and aren't the jealous type. Ex-girlfriends will call him, so make sure you're confident enough to handle the extra attention this Prince Charming will receive.

The Sagittarius Girl

The Sag girl likes her independence. She is honest and direct, and seldom does she take tips from fashion magazines. She's got her own style. To woo an Archer gal, you must be someone who will bring more excitement into her life. She already has tons of friends and a hectic schedule. She needs someone who can add something to her life. Being athletic is a plus because this gal has a sporty side. If you look hot in a pair of blue jeans and a crisp, white T-shirt, you get extra points. Keep complaints and your antidepressants to yourself. This lady looks at everything in a positive light. Ms. Sagittarius is looking for a hot date, a best friend, and a confidante, all wrapped up into one package. Don't ever make her feel trapped, attempt to smother her, or tell her what she's going to do. She'll bolt for the nearest exit sign. Keep her laughing. A sense of humor goes a long way with this lady.

Sagittarius with Sagittarius

If their brutal honesty doesn't kill the relationship, the two Archers may have a good thing. If the flames burn out, both have the sense to move on to greener pastures without hesitation and long, overdrawn goodbyes. Usually the couple can work through any problem because of their positive natures. "Nothing is as bad as it seems" and "things will be better tomorrow" are mottoes Sagittarians live by. You understand each other so well and enjoy the same things that if a dating relationship doesn't last, a friendship certainly can!

♥ ♥ ♥ Attraction

♥ ♥ ♥ ♥ ♥ Compatibility

♥ ♥ ♥ ♥ Communication

♥ ♥ ♥ ♥ ♥ Friendship

♥ ♥ ♥ ♥ ♥ Marriage Material

Would Lucas Black ever date Katie Holmes?

Sagittarius with Capricorn

Sagittarians fight to break the very restraints and traditions that Capricorns work to build. The two may enjoy each other's company and no-nonsense approach to life, but there is no place for the freedom-loving Sagittarius in Capricorn's organized world.

Sag wouldn't want to live there too long anyway. There are too many places to see, people to meet, and hearts to conquer. Capricorn will never understand Sagittarius' wanderlust, but will secretly envy it. This is not a "till death do us part" kind of love.

♥ ♥ ♥ Attraction

♥ Compatibility

♥ ♥ Communication

♥ ♥ ♥ ♥ Friendship

♥ Marriage Material

What about Aaron Carter and Amber Benson hanging out together?

Sagittarius with Aquarius

Here we have two freedom-loving truth seekers. They both hate to be tied down and will try anything once. Sagittarius and Aquarius are a great match! They talk psychic stuff and meditate together. Aquarius expects loyalty. So if the Sagittarius is really ready to make that kind of commitment, Aquarius should jump at the chance. Their friendship and romance will be one they'll never forget!

♥ ♥ ♥ ♥ Attraction

♥ ♥ ♥ ♥ ♥ Compatibility

♥ ♥ ♥ ♥ Communication

♥ ♥ ♥ ♥ ♥ Friendship

♥ ♥ ♥ ♥ Marriage Material

Here's a great couple: Brad Pitt and Jennifer Aniston.

Sagittarius with Pisces

Pisces need to smother their partners with lots of attention. This may hinder a relationship with a Sagittarius. The roaming Archer wants to be free or at least feel as if no one is tying him or her down. Pisces will feel that they're not appreciated and that Sag doesn't care about them at all. That may not be true, but the Fish's constant need for attention will give an Archer justification to run. They won't see eye to eye.

♥ ♥ Attraction

♥ Compatibility

♥ Communication

♥ ♥ Friendship

♥ Marriage Material

Can you see Ben Stiller with Chelsea Clinton?

Sagittarius with Aries

While some signs may find Aries too aggressive and bold for their tastes, Sagittarius adores what Aries can bring to a relationship. The Archer and the Ram agree on a lot of things. They both feel that a person should take risks in life and that nothing is impossible! They share a love of knowledge and spirituality, so they'll allow one another to take turns playing the roles of teacher and student.

♥ ♥ ♥ ♥ Attraction

♥ ♥ ♥ ♥ Compatibility

♥ ♥ ♥ ♥ Communication

♥ ♥ ♥ ♥ ♥ Friendship

♥ ♥ ♥ ♥ ♥ Marriage Material

Christina Aguilera meets Heath Ledger.

Sagittarius with Taurus

That Sagittarius charm initially draws the Taurus, but there's not much else to hold this relationship together. When the Bull's possessive side comes charging out, Sag will have no choice but to run. Sagittarians favor their personal freedom over love, although they'd like to keep both. They aren't going to let anyone fence them in. The famous Taurus temper is also something they won't tolerate. I wouldn't bet on this relationship lasting.

- ♥ ♥ Attraction
- ♥ ♥ Compatibility
- ♥ ♥ Communication
- ♥ ♥ ♥ Friendship
- ♥ Marriage Material

Consider Frankie Muniz with Holly Valance.

Sagittarius with Gemini

The Archer and the Twins take their time getting to know one another, but when they do, they can be friends forever! This is a case of opposite attraction, but you'd be surprised at how much they have in common. Both are flirty and fun. This couple can't stand to be bored, so they'll always find some new mountains to climb and interesting ways to spend time together. The communication lines are always open to one another. Go for it!

- ♥ ♥ ♥ ♥ Attraction
- ♥ ♥ ♥ ♥ Compatibility
- ♥ ♥ ♥ ♥ Communication
- ♥ ♥ ♥ ♥ Friendship
- ♥ ♥ ♥ ♥ Marriage Material

Alyssa Milano and Prince William?

Sagittarius and Cancer

Their souls connect. Their eyes meet. They are drawn to one another across the crowded room. The Sagittarius/Cancer love affair offers romance novelists great material. However, this couple would be better off reading the book than living it. Most of these connections don't end happily ever after. This is very confusing because the initial attraction is so strong: Sag and Cancer are like two magnets. They can't stay away from one another. Eventually, the Crab's need to settle down will suffocate the freedom-loving Archer. Arguments are par for the course. The relationship is on and off for months, even years, until both realize that it doesn't meet their individual needs.

♥ ♥ ♥ Attraction
♥ ♥ Compatibility
♥ ♥ Communication
♥ ♥ ♥ Friendship
♥ ♥ Marriage Material

Raven and David Spade.

Sagittarius and Leo

These two love to have fun. They live in the moment and dream big! This is a relationship that will never grow dull. Sag and Leo are considered the luckiest signs in the zodiac. Put them together and what amazing good fortune they'll have! Leos may need to curb their bossy tendencies. Sagittarians need to be gentle when dealing with Leo's ego. They are very honest and blunt, and not afraid to point out a Lion's flaws. The biggest concern is overindulgence. Leo and Sagittarius do nothing halfway. It's usually to the extreme. They believe in living life to the fullest, and often on the edge!

♥ ♥ ♥ ♥ Attraction
♥ ♥ ♥ ♥ Compatibility
♥ ♥ ♥ ♥ Communication
♥ ♥ ♥ ♥ Friendship
♥ ♥ ♥ ♥ ♥ Marriage Material

Britney Spears and Matt LeBlanc?

Sagittarius with Virgo

Let's look at an ordinary week in the life of Sagittarius and Virgo. There are seven days in the week. The first three days are just wonderful. Things run smoothly. The couple is in love. They laugh. They talk. Then the fourth day hits. It's downhill from there. Little arguments start. They pick on one another. They can't stand to be in the same room together! The battle lines are drawn. The less time these two spend together, the longer the relationship will last. It's that simple.

- ♥ ♥ Attraction
- ♥ Compatibility
- ♥ Communication
- ♥ ♥ ♥ Friendship
- ♥ Marriage Material

Brad Pitt and Shania Twain?

Sagittarius with Libra

I give this match two thumbs up! If for some reason there is a breakup, this couple will get a second chance. They could find their way back to one another! Sagittarians are hard to tie down. They need to get their wanderlust out of their systems before they date someone seriously. Libras, on the other hand, have been waiting to fall in love all of their lives. These two can enjoy a great relationship. But the timing has to be right. When Sagittarians have had their fill of life's curiosities, they will likely come back for Libra. Hopefully, the Archer won't make the Libra wait too long.

- ♥ ♥ ♥ ♥ Attraction
- ♥ ♥ ♥ Compatibility
- ♥ ♥ ♥ ♥ Communication
- ♥ ♥ ♥ ♥ Friendship
- ♥ ♥ ♥ ♥ ♥ Marriage Material

How about Brendan Fraser and Alicia Silverstone?

Sagittarius with Scorpio

Usually crisis brings couples closer together. In the Sagittarius/Scorpio relationship, crisis could pull them apart. This relationship will have more than its share of problems. Each sun sign deals with problems in different ways. Scorpios want answers immediately. They are intense and emotional. Sagittarians are apt to take a lighthearted approach to issues that Scorpios hold dear. Issues of jealousy and loyalty will likely come up. There is passion, but the flames may die out if Scorpio's emotional needs don't get met.

♥ ♥ Attraction

♥ ♥ Compatibility

♥ ♥ Communication

♥ ♥ ♥ Friendship

♥ ♥ Marriage Material

It didn't work with Benjamin Bratt and Julia Roberts!

What a Sagittarius Is Looking for in Love

Sagittarians want a best friend who they can be themselves with. They want someone who is honest and not afraid to speak the truth. They like a bold girl or a confident guy. They're looking for someone who will work out with them at the gym, cheer their favorite sports team to victory, and won't ask them where they've been. If you give a Sag some personal space, act like you really don't need him or her and that your happiness doesn't depend solely on him or her, the Sag will want you even more!

First Date Idea

A sporting event, a car show, Starbucks, and any place where they can strike up a conversation with a crowd works best for a first date. Since they are people lovers, their motto is "the more the merrier." You won't have to spend a month's allowance on a date, just make sure it includes several fun things to do. You could go horseback riding or plan a trip to the museum to see the latest archaeological finds. An outdoor concert suits them just fine, or a scenic drive along the beach with the top down and the radio blaring to their favorite station.

The Dumped Sagittarius

The dumped Sag will rebound in no time. "No use crying over spilled milk," the Sag will say. Sagittarians are positive thinkers and know the universe will introduce them to someone else very soon . . . or they'll ask out that person they've been flirting with. There's always a skeleton in the Archer's closet, someone from the past, who's waiting for a second chance. They won't be alone for long unless they want to be!

How to Attract a Sagittarius

- Be positive and outgoing
- Have a passion for sports
- Drive a cool car
- Wear the color purple
- Talk about politics, religion, and different philosophies

Never Ever

- Smother a Sag
- Be dishonest
- Be negative
- Expect fidelity
- Boss him or her around

Capricorn
The Goat
December 23–January 20

Cool Crushes: Taurus and Virgo

Opposite Attraction: Cancer

Fast Fizzles: Aries and Libra

Best Buds: Scorpio and Pisces

Heartbreakers: Gemini and Leo

Past Life Connection: Sagittarius

Lucky in Love Months: May and July

Capricorn are cautious when it comes to love. It may take them months and sometimes years to ask for a date. It is important for them to know that they won't be turned down. When they do finally get around to dating, they mean serious business. The evening is impeccably planned out, far in advance. Cappys are organized people. They always wear watches. Expect them to be early rather than on time. Capricorn look for boyfriends and girlfriends they think "have it all together." Social status is very important. They like to date the guys and gals who are considered popular, like the sports hero, the valedictorian, or the prom queen. This is not to say that the old Goats are snobby; they just want their peers to look up to them. They are serious creatures. Emotional people scare them, but ironically, they draw these types to them. Capricorn are hard workers. Some get part-time jobs in their freshman year, so romance is not high on their list of priorities. That's why you may get mixed signals from them. Their logical, stoic personalities don't always make for good romance. But they can be very convincing when attracted to someone. These are the strong, dependable types. They don't bend easily. They are not as bullheaded as Taurus or as unyielding as Scorpio, but Cappys will stand their ground if the cause is right. They are very direct people, too. Capricorns speak their minds. They don't hold much back. If you ask a question, expect an honest, direct answer. If a Goat asks you out, he or she is serious about you. If the first evening out goes well, you may find yourself with a date every Friday night. Honesty, stability, and old-fashioned values are what the Capricorn can bring to a relationship. If you're not into all of that mushy stuff, the Goat will make a wonderful partner!

The Capricorn Guy

Capricorn guys are the strong, silent types, but beneath their cool exterior is a prince who really wants to find his princess and fall in love. To capture his attention, you should act very ladylike and a bit conservative. Show him that you are traditional and loyal. Being the very best you can be makes him all the more interested. Allow him to be the "man" in the relationship, but don't let him get away with bossing you around. Cappy likes to be in charge. Know that he's serious and not as emotional as other zodiac signs. Don't pressure him to talk about his feelings. Sometimes he appears cheap. He thinks of himself as thrifty and a good money manager. He's a logical type and pretty smart. He probably has a good idea of what he wants to do after graduation: college and a business degree of some sort are in his future. Gain his trust and respect, and the rest is easy. He's looking for a long-term commitment. Even though he is cautious about letting his heart get the best of him, he does want to meet the girl of his dreams. Could it be you?

The Capricorn Girl

She's a no-nonsense, mature, matter-of-fact lady who knows what she wants and goes after it. She's down-to-earth and can be extremely cautious about getting involved with someone. But once a Capricorn gal falls in love, it's usually for keeps. She appreciates the finer things in life. Her standards are very high. You'll have to prove yourself over and over again. But it's worth the effort because Capricorns are loyal and dependable. Control your temper around her. Don't swear. Act mature. Oh yes, you should have some sort of income: establish a trust fund or make decent wages at a part time job. Be honest. Talk about your plans for the future and how you intend to be rich and successful. If you're a mess or a big flirt, if you flunk math or have a lot of "baggage" from past relationships, you don't stand a chance with this Goat.

Capricorn with Capricorn

Both of you are hard workers and are very mature for your age. You admire one another's drive and ambition. However, your schedule is so jam-packed with activities and responsibilities, will you ever get together? If you make time for one another, this will be a great relationship. Goats are very strong-willed creatures, though. If they disagree with you about something, they will not budge easily from their stance. But your logical way of looking at things will help you work on any love crises that may arise.

   ♥ ♥ ♥ Attraction
   ♥ ♥ ♥ ♥ Compatibility
   ♥ ♥ ♥ ♥ Communication
   ♥ ♥ ♥ ♥ Friendship
   ♥ ♥ ♥ ♥ ♥ Marriage Material

Cuba Gooding, Jr. and Jessica Andrews.

Capricorn with Aquarius

The Aquarius new age ideals will clash with the traditional ways of the Capricorn. Aquarians seek change and are constantly looking toward the future. Capricorns hang on tightly to the past. Their tastes are worlds apart. The Goat favors Gucci. The Water Bearer may sport the latest fads, like tattoos, body piercings, and funky haircuts, complete with colored highlights!

   ♥ ♥ Attraction
   ♥ ♥ Compatibility
   ♥ ♥ ♥ Communication
   ♥ ♥ ♥ ♥ Friendship
   ♥ ♥ Marriage Material

Nicholas Cage and Lisa Marie Presley didn't last.

Capricorn with Pisces

Pisces will help Capricorn lighten up and laugh more, and will open the Cappy's world to dreams, romance, and fantasy. It may take a little nudging on the part of the Fish, but the Goat will find the Pisces personality a nice retreat after a long day at school. Pisces can help Capricorn relax and not look at the world too seriously. Capricorn can help bring Pisces back down to earth if he or she wanders too far from reality. Their spirits intertwine. Generally, this combination works if the two look at each other as unique rather than "strange."

- ♥ ♥ ♥ Attraction
- ♥ ♥ ♥ Compatibility
- ♥ ♥ ♥ Communication
- ♥ ♥ ♥ ♥ Friendship
- ♥ ♥ ♥ ♥ Marriage Material

Could you see Amber Benson and Julio Iglesias, Jr. on a date?

Capricorn with Aries

Things move way too fast in this relationship for Capricorn. Cappy doesn't approve of Aries' pushy, impractical attitude. Aries won't wait around for anything or anyone! Aries is too much for Capricorn to handle. The cautious Goat needs to sit and think before making a decision. Aries doesn't take time to consider options. Rams need to take action! One partner is always one step ahead or one step behind.

- ♥ ♥ Attraction
- ♥ Compatibility
- ♥ ♥ Communication
- ♥ ♥ ♥ Friendship
- ♥ Marriage Material

How about Jim Carrey and Amanda Bynes?

Capricorn with Taurus

These two earth signs have what it takes to make a relationship work. Their basic needs are the same. They are actually quite alike. Oh, there'll be arguments because both signs are strong-willed and have a tendency to be bossy. Hardworking Capricorn may find Taurus a little lazy when it comes to getting homework completed on time, and the Bulls may resent the Goats for having their dates all planned out without their input. A little spontaneity isn't so bad, you know. Other than that, the relationship is very comfortable.

♥ ♥ ♥ ♥   Attraction

♥ ♥ ♥ ♥ ♥   Compatibility

♥ ♥ ♥ ♥   Communication

♥ ♥ ♥ ♥   Friendship

♥ ♥ ♥ ♥ ♥   Marriage Material

Think about Tiger Woods and Jessica Alba.

Capricorn with Gemini

Since Capricorns represent the mature, responsible, old sign of the zodiac, it's hard for Goats to live in youthful Gemini's fun-loving world. They can offer each other a fresh way of looking at things, but there are so many differences to contend with. Flexible Gemini is more apt to share ideas. Geminis are used to looking at both sides of a coin. However, Capricorn is very opinionated and may feel Gemini's views are just a waste of his or her valuable time.

♥ ♥   Attraction

♥   Compatibility

♥ ♥   Communication

♥ ♥ ♥   Friendship

♥   Marriage Material

Consider Josh Evans and Alanis Morissette!

Capricorn with Cancer

This combination either works wonderfully or not at all. It helps if both parties understand that they are completely opposite types. There's a magnetic pull between the two of them. Tons of attraction! Heavy chemistry! Can it last? A lot depends on whether or not they are willing to meet each other halfway. Because of Cancer's fragile feelings, Capricorn needs to be extra sensitive. The Goat's brutal honesty doesn't sit well with moon children. Understand that the cool exterior of the Capricorn doesn't melt for many. However, Cancer is one sign that has the power to soften up the old goat.

♥ ♥ ♥ ♥ ♥ Attraction
♥ ♥ ♥ Compatibility
♥ ♥ ♥ Communication
♥ ♥ ♥ Friendship
♥ ♥ ♥ ♥ Marriage Material

You know the story of Kid Rock and Pamela Anderson.

Capricorn with Leo

The Goat and the Lion are always striving to be the best they can be. That much they do have in common. But reserved Cappys don't approve of Leo's flashy ways or how Leos spend their money so freely. Lions may consider Goats to be cheap tightwads, but they'll certainly respect them for their brains and ambition. Best buddies? Yes! Going steady? No!

♥ ♥ Attraction
♥ ♥ Compatibility
♥ ♥ Communication
♥ ♥ ♥ Friendship
♥ ♥ Marriage Material

Will Ricky Martin and Charlize Theron ever meet up?

Capricorn with Virgo

The Capricorn/Virgo relationship works like a charm. One is logical and the other is analytical. Gosh, things could get a little boring! They understand each other's thoughts and feelings. When problems arise, these two will talk them out. Their friends may find more passion and excitement in their dating experiences, but the Cappy and Virgo have stability and a long, happy future ahead.

♥ ♥ ♥ ♥   Attraction
♥ ♥ ♥ ♥ ♥   Compatibility
♥ ♥ ♥ ♥   Communication
♥ ♥ ♥ ♥   Friendship
♥ ♥ ♥ ♥ ♥   Marriage Material

Does January Jones have time for Paul Walker in her busy schedule?

Capricorn with Libra

Save yourself some time and tears, Capricorn. Look elsewhere for love. On the surface, this relationship looks promising. Capricorn and Libra enjoy nice things, designer fashions, and are concerned with social status. However, these two will be at odds over their free time. Their hobbies and interests are different. Social Libra may want to party and dance all night long. Capricorn thinks early to bed, early to rise. If a balance is not struck between the two, they'll go off in different directions.

♥ ♥ ♥   Attraction
♥ ♥   Compatibility
♥ ♥   Communication
♥ ♥   Friendship
♥   Marriage Material

Would Tiger Woods and Rachael Leigh Cook get along?

Capricorn with Scorpio

Capricorn and Scorpio are private people. Reserved, quiet, and sometimes aloof, this couple has staying power. They enjoy each other's company, but Scorpio's need to control everything is no match for the Goat. The Goats are very logical in love. Seldom do they understand the depth of a Scorpio's emotions. If they agree to meet in the middle, this could be a wonderful and long-lasting relationship. Give it a try!

♥ ♥ ♥ ♥ Attraction
♥ ♥ ♥ ♥ Compatibility
♥ ♥ ♥ Communication
♥ ♥ ♥ ♥ Friendship
♥ ♥ ♥ ♥ Marriage Material

Will there ever be true love between Erin Cahill and Ryan Gosling?

Capricorn with Sagittarius

This isn't one of the best combinations for love. This relationship will have a short fuse. Since both signs enjoy a good debate, communication presents no problem, but the chemistry is not strong. Freedom-loving Sagittarius breaks tradition too much for Capricorn to feel safe. Capricorns are always on time for dates. They often arrive early. Sagittarians are notoriously late. They're messy, too. Sagittarians don't mind clutter. They're known to have the messiest rooms ever! Tidy Capricorn has a place for everything. If these two decide to make a go of it, Capricorn will have to loosen up a little. Sagittarius will have to buy a watch!

♥ ♥ Attraction
♥ ♥ Compatibility
♥ ♥ ♥ Communication
♥ ♥ ♥ ♥ Friendship
♥ ♥ Marriage Material

How about Johnny de Mol and Jennifer Connelly getting together? Do you see it?

What a Capricorn Is Looking for in Love

Cappys are looking for a loyal, trustworthy guy or gal who would never embarrass them in public. They want someone who is popular and respected by his or her friends. Cappys like people who are ambitious and plan ahead. If you've got your eye on a college scholarship or plan on entering law school, then the Cappy will make time to talk to you! No flashy, arrogant "know it alls" will do. Goats like easygoing and down-to-earth types who are mature for their age and have set goals for the future. If your car is trashed and littered with fast food wrappers, better give it a good cleanup before you even think of picking a Goat up for date. A Goat will simply refuse to soil his or her designer duds in a messy car.

First Date Ideas

If you're on a limited budget and can't afford much, choose one activity and blow your entire stash on that. An elegant dinner for two overlooking the city's streetscape would impress the Goat. An afternoon spent in your city's cultural center, wandering through art museums and the planetarium is another option. A day swimming, hiking, or bicycling is fun. Make sure your date is well organized and that you're on time to pick the Capricorn up!

The Dumped Capricorn

Dumped Cappys will act like everything is fine. Underneath their calm exterior they probably care very much, but they won't show you their emotional side. They're cautious about falling in love, so don't expect a Capricorn to get back in the dating game right away. It will take time for the Cappy's heart to heal. Goats will look at the breakup from a logical level, but expect them to shed a few tears in private when no one is looking.

How to Attract a Capricorn

- Dress well

- Talk about your big plans for the future

- Show off your intelligent side

- Be polite and kind

- Ask for his or her opinion

Never Ever

- Be a loud mouth

- Embarrass the Cappy

- Be emotionally needy

- Criticize the way the Capricorn dresses or looks

- Pressure the Cappy to go out when he or she needs to study or work

Aquarius
The Water Bearer
January 21–February 19

Cool Crushes: Aries and Gemini

Opposite Attraction: Leo

Fast Fizzles: Cancer and Scorpio

Best Buds: Sagittarius and Libra

Heartbreakers: Taurus and Virgo

Past Life Connection: Capricorn

Lucky in Love Months: June and August

Aquarius teens are unique and eccentric individuals. They seem to be living ahead of the times, with visions of the way the future should be. They love to invent and create things. Many are fond of the latest gadgets and gizmos, and are computer whizzes. Friendship are most important to those born under the sign of the Water Bearer. They make their friends their family. Because Aquarians get bored easily, they are constantly looking for new adventures or mountains to climb. They tire easily of the same old routine. Unfortunately, this holds true in the area of romance, too. Hopefully, if you're attracted to one of these dear hearts, you love to try new things and won't allow the relationship to grow stagnant.

Another tidbit you should know: Aquarians are not big criers and weepers. They are intellectual beings and at times can appear to shut their feelings off completely. If you end a relationship with an Aquarius, he or she will act like it's no big deal. If there's a crisis, he or she will appear unmoved. But underneath that cool, aloof exterior is a heart of gold. Aquarians love the new age, so if you're open to getting your tarot cards read, you win extra points! If you're surfing the web, there's bound to be an Aquarius in your chat room. Many times you will find Aquarians spearheading fundraisers and causes. They enjoy large groups rather than intimate gatherings. They look for love among their friends and those whose deepest desire is to make the world a better place. Aquarians expect equality in a relationship. They love deeply when the right guy or girl comes along. The way to enjoy a relationship with an Aquarian is to let the person be who he or she is. Don't try to change him or her. Support his or her goals and dreams. Most of all, be the Aquarian's best friend.

The Aquarius Guy

The Aquarius guy is a "know it all." He is intelligent and has an opinion on everything. If you want to win his heart, let him talk and make him feel that what he has to say is very important. Here's a guy who appreciates his freedom, so don't pressure him into a commitment or be overly demanding of his time. There are two types of Aquarius: extroverted and introverted. If yours is friendly and outgoing, you may have to compete for his time and attention with the many friends he has. Join in his group and learn to love his quirky buddies. If he's the quiet type, give him space when he needs it. You must be willing to try new adventures with both types of guys. How about sky diving, perhaps, or mountain climbing? Did you know you're interested in a computer genius? Make sure you have an e-mail address so you can communicate more often. Aquarians are known to spend hours online. This is a "tough" guy, so don't do anything that would make him look foolish, feminine, or less than the macho man he is! He hates being told what to do. Be kind, gentle, and a little bit of a risk taker, and you'll find a love match.

The Aquarius Girl

She's a free spirit, and devoted to her causes and friends. If she can fit you in her busy schedule, great! If not, you'll have to prove worthy of her precious time. The best way to woo her is to be her friend first. Have conversations about astrology, current events, and deep topics. She'll be direct with words, so don't mince yours. She likes a strong, self-assured guy with a tender side. Show her both. She craves change, so whatever you do, don't get stuck in a boring dating routine. Make sure to live it up every weekend. Try new things. Take her to places she's never been before. Don't be passive or jealous. Forget mind games and playing hard to get. Honesty with an Aquarius gal is always the best policy. Keep things interesting. Surprise her. She's not into money as much as she's into security and honesty. If she can talk to you about anything and feels you're her very best friend, you'll conquer her heart!

Aquarius with Aquarius

If both are working toward the same goals, this duo can expect great happiness. They understand the need for change. Life will never be boring. You'll try the latest restaurants, hairstyles, and fads. Pets will be treated like royal members of the family. Friends who drop by to visit could find the hospitality so inviting that they will stay way past their welcome.

- ♥ ♥ ♥ Attraction
- ♥ ♥ ♥ ♥ Compatibility
- ♥ ♥ ♥ ♥ Communication
- ♥ ♥ ♥ ♥ Friendship
- ♥ ♥ ♥ ♥ Marriage Material

Consider Ashton Kutcher and Alicia Keys.

Aquarius with Pisces

If these two make it past the first date, then a relationship has potential. Aquarius and Pisces communicate so differently. Pisces could find Aquarius condescending. Aquarius may say Pisces is too shallow. The first date will lay the basis for who's in control of this relationship. Sometimes Pisces may feel left out around all of Aquarius' friends. Pisces want to explore their romantic dreams, and Aquarians are technical when it comes to the theory of love. Aquarius will grow bored or tired of the smothering Pisces' constant need for reassurance. Just be friends.

♥ ♥ Attraction
♥ ♥ Compatibility
♥ ♥ Communication
♥ ♥ ♥ ♥ Friendship
♥ ♥ Marriage Material

How about Seth Green meeting Jenny Thompson?

Aquarius with Aries

Here's a good gamble. Aries are willing to try anything once. They are strong, self-assured, and have lots to say. Aquarius will appreciate the positive, upbeat personality of the Ram. When these two argue, they will fight fair, but there will often be no resolution because both signs are the "know it alls" of the zodiac. They can learn a lot from one another if they just listen. Aries demand to be number one. With Aquarius, they'll never have to ask for admiration or support. It'll be right there. In turn, Aries will encourage the Water Bearer to go after his or her wildest dreams.

♥ ♥ ♥ ♥ ♥ Attraction
♥ ♥ ♥ ♥ Compatibility
♥ ♥ ♥ ♥ Communication
♥ ♥ ♥ ♥ Friendship
♥ ♥ ♥ ♥ Marriage Material

How about Vince Carter and Mandy Moore getting together?

Aquarius with Taurus

Fun to flirt with, but not to date! Disappointment will be no stranger to this relationship. Taurus and Aquarius are fixed signs. They don't bend easily. Taurus won't like the fact that Aquarius' schedule is *so* busy. The Water Bearer doesn't spend enough time with the Bull, who craves affection and attention. Aquarians love to be where the action is. They feel alive and connected to the universe when they are with their friends. Taureans prefer spending time alone with those they love. They don't want to share you with anyone! Sometimes differences in a relationship are healthy, but here they could prove otherwise.

♥ ♥ Attraction
♥ Compatibility
♥ ♥ Communication
♥ ♥ ♥ Friendship
♥ Marriage Material

Would Sarah McLachlan ever date Billy Crawford?

Aquarius with Gemini

The energy between these two air signs flows nicely. The Aquarius and Gemini can talk nonsense for hours! If there's serious business to discuss, these quick minds will work together to get the job done. Power struggles are few and far between. Friends are welcome any time, day or night. Attraction can last through the years because both are willing to pursue their own individual goals, and this keeps the relationship fresh and exciting. Although the word "forever" isn't in their vocabulary, Aquarius and Gemini do agree never to say "never."

♥ ♥ ♥ ♥ Attraction
♥ ♥ ♥ ♥ ♥ Compatibility
♥ ♥ ♥ ♥ Communication
♥ ♥ ♥ ♥ Friendship
♥ ♥ ♥ ♥ ♥ Marriage Material

Imagine Christian Bale and Steffi Graff on a date!

Aquarius with Cancer

Some astrology books claim this relationship has potential. In my practice, it has proven to be one of the most difficult to maintain. These two could really be attracted to their differences at first, but those differences could break them apart.

Aquarians cannot give the moody Cancers the emotional security they need. Home- and family-loving Crabs cannot give Aquarians the freedom they need to make sweeping changes in their lives. Both have completely different purposes to fulfill. It's very likely that Aquarians are not interested in the things that Cancers hold most dear. Here's the answer: since Aquarians treat their friends like Cancers treat their families, Cancer and Aquarius, just be friends!

- ♥ Attraction
- ♥ Compatibility
- ♥ ♥ Communication
- ♥ ♥ ♥ Friendship
- ♥ Marriage Material

Would Portia de Rossi like Tobey McGuire?

Aquarius with Leo

They are opposites but possess some of the same strong desires and goals. Both have big hearts but show them off in different ways. The Leo heart will be generous when in love. Leo showers the object of his or her affection with lots of cool gifts and special attention. The Aquarius heart is big when it comes to helping the world. Aquarians give to the less fortunate and underprivileged. They can learn a lot from one another. Leos can learn that the power of love comes back when you give love away. The more people you touch, the more your life will be blessed. Aquarius can learn through Leo that just one single relationship can enrich your life in an amazing way! On the downside, the bossy Lion may try to control the Water Bearer. If that's the case, Aquarius won't hang around too long.

- ♥ ♥ ♥ ♥ Attraction
- ♥ ♥ ♥ Compatibility
- ♥ ♥ ♥ Communication
- ♥ ♥ ♥ ♥ Friendship
- ♥ ♥ ♥ Marriage Material

Kelly Rowland and Matthew Perry?

Aquarius with Virgo

Both have strong minds, but Virgo may not feel Aquarius is very practical. The Water Bearer's insightful futuristic ideas may not jive with Virgo's sensible approach to life and love. Aquarius doesn't care to hear about the mundane, but Virgo has planned out every little detail of their Saturday night date. Never mind if Aquarius has plans with the gang. Compromise is the only way this relationship can survive. Better move on!

♥ ♥ Attraction
♥ ♥ Compatibility
♥ ♥ ♥ Communication
♥ ♥ ♥ Friendship
♥ ♥ Marriage Material

Why wouldn't Justin Timberlake think Beyoncé Knowles is beautiful?

Aquarius with Libra

The potential for happiness is strong with these lovebirds. Libra won't pout like other signs when Aquarius changes the weekend game plan. Just as long as Libra is part of those changes, all will be fine! The intellectual and creative energies these two possess is a turn-on. Libra can bring balance to Aquarius' erratic life. Friends are like family here, and socializing is a big part of their relationship.

♥ ♥ ♥ ♥ Attraction
♥ ♥ ♥ ♥ Compatibility
♥ ♥ ♥ ♥ Communication
♥ ♥ ♥ ♥ Friendship
♥ ♥ ♥ ♥ ♥ Marriage Material

Imagine Johnny Diaz Reyes along with Neve Campbell.

Aquarius with Scorpio

The Aquarians can handle almost anything that's thrown their way. But it's unlikely that they'll be able to handle a relationship with a Scorpio. Don't even try, Aquarius. The intense Scorpio will not allow you to get your way. There'll be no changes without Scorpio's approval. Scorpio will make you pay if you try to do anything sneaky. So why waste your energy? Scorpios may be jealous of time spent with friends. There's constant bickering. Take an aspirin and move on!

- ♥ ♥ ♥ Attraction
- ♥ Compatibility
- ♥ Communication
- ♥ ♥ Friendship
- ♥ Marriage Material

Do you recall when Ashton Kutcher and Brittany Murphy were an item?

Aquarius with Sagittarius

What a delightful match! Aquarius and Sagittarius can enrich each other's lives. They have much to share. Both are determined to make the best of whatever life hands them. They are willing to grab the brass ring, and they do it with such passion that it spills over into their relationship. This couple's calendar will be filled with fun activities and plans with friends. If Sagittarius is mature, then expect longevity in this relationship. If not, the romance will be marked by highs and lows, but it will still be a very special one.

- ♥ ♥ ♥ ♥ Attraction
- ♥ ♥ ♥ ♥ ♥ Compatibility
- ♥ ♥ ♥ ♥ Communication
- ♥ ♥ ♥ ♥ Friendship
- ♥ ♥ ♥ ♥ Marriage Material

Remember the Justin Timberlake and Britney Spears dating days?

Aquarius with Capricorn

The tried and true works well for cautious Capricorn. The Aquarius hopes to break from tradition and try new things. There's a definite clash of ideas when these two get together. Capricorns will not find the stability they are looking for here. They must learn to "expect the unexpected" if they want to stay with the Water Bearer. Aquarians could feel restricted in this commitment, never finding the freedom necessary to be true to themselves.

- ♥ ♥ Attraction
- ♥ ♥ Compatibility
- ♥ ♥ Communication
- ♥ ♥ ♥ Friendship
- ♥ ♥ Marriage Material

Would Lisa Marie Presley and Shawn Wayans see eye to eye?

What an Aquarius Is Looking for in Love

Water Bearers are looking for a best buddy—someone who will give them unconditional love and allow them to be themselves. The perfect choice for an Aquarius is a soul mate who has a strong desire to help make the world a better place, just as the Aquarius does. Water Bearers want someone who won't fence them in, who is unique and not afraid to be "different," and who doesn't follow the crowd but creates his or her own place in the sun.

First Date Ideas

Go wherever there's a crowd. To an Aquarius, the more the merrier. Take him or her to a friend's party or a dance, or go to a coffee shop to catch up on the latest gossip and buzz going around school. Make sure you don't stay too long anywhere unless the Water Bearer agrees, as he or she gets bored easily. Try to plan several activities that you know the Aquarius likes. Outdoor activities are always good choices too: go hiking, biking, or shoot hoops.

The Dumped Aquarius

Dumped Aquarians will have plenty of friends around to cheer them up. Don't worry about them brooding for weeks. According to the Water Bearer, there's no use crying over spilled milk. They tend to intellectualize their feelings. It's a good bet they didn't get too emotionally involved with you in the first place. They'll date again when the time is right . . . but for now, they'll enjoy just hanging out with their best buds.

How to Attract an Aquarius

- Be unique

- Act friendly

- Speak up for what you believe in

- Have an "attitude" (Aquarius will read that as confident and self-assured)

- Get involved in group activities that make a difference

Never Ever

- Criticize an Aquarian's friends

- Tie him or her down

- Expect him or her to change

- Expect an Aquarius to be on time

- Be boring

Pisces
The Fish
February 20–March 20

Cool Crushes: Taurus and Cancer

Opposite Attraction: Virgo

Fast Fizzles: Gemini and Sagittarius

Best Buds: Capricorn and Scorpio

Heartbreakers: Aries and Libra

Past Life Connection: Aquarius

Lucky in Love Months: July and September

If you meet someone with the most beautiful crystal-blue eyes, you've probably met a Pisces. Pisces believe in fairy tales that end happily ever after. They are the dreamers of the zodiac. They love to be in love. Fantasy plays a big part in their love lives. Pisces are gentle, spiritual creatures who live to please those they love. They will go to the ends of the earth to make sure their boyfriend or girlfriend is happy.

They are also very intuitive, and their dreams can be prophetic. I always tell my Pisces clients to listen to their dreams and learn how to interpret them. A Pisces could dream of a someone special coming into his or her life, and weeks later, that special person could turn out to be you!

These are very sympathetic creatures. Pisces carry the weight of the world on their backs. They feel guilty about everything. They feel sorry for everyone. Fish also have a tendency to smother those they love. For freedom-loving signs, that could be a little too much lovin'. All Pisces have a positive and negative side. When they get into their famous pity parties, they can stay there for weeks. But if they deny their emotional feelings, they will need to be careful not to use escapism to cope (for example, they may lock themselves in their rooms for days on end). On the positive side, they are caring and helpful. Pisces make great friends and loyal comrades. Maybe they whine too much, dream too much, and some say they love too much, but that's not so terrible, now, is it?

The Pisces Guy

He can be the most romantic guy you've ever met or the most utterly impossible. Pisces guys at their best are kind, gentle, intuitive, and dreamy. At their worst, they complain, whine, and get depressed. If you've already fallen head over heels for a Fish, here's what you do: get romantic, too. Spend hours with him, making memories. He wants to spend all of his free time with you! Watch sunsets together. Talk about his dreams and fantasies. Be his cheerleader in life, but not his enabler or addiction. Bring some structure into his world, because he needs it badly. Make plans and schedules and stick to them. Let him know you'll be there through thick and thin. Be someone Pisces can depend on. He may try to smother you. If you like your independence, you may have to give up a little private time to please him.

The Pisces Girl

This gal loves to please! The needier you are, the better! She loves to feel as if she is your "everything." She will stick by you through whatever crises come your way. The Pisces girl is very psychic, yet sometimes very insecure, so you must make her always feel safe and emotionally secure in a relationship. The little things you do, she'll remember. Write her a love letter. Buy her a rose. Give her a box of candy to delight her sweet tooth. She loves romance and probably has been dreaming of Prince Charming all of her life. Be her knight in shining armor; someone she can lean on and share her fears and sorrows with. She's been searching for her soul mate for years. Discover your past lives together. Take her to romantic, weepy movies. Find a breathtaking view at a park, waterfall, or mountainside: a spot she can call "our special place." Anything you do to romance this lady will win you points. She's not interested in money as much as she is interested in your heart. Make her feel like a princess. Any effort you put forth to make this relationship magical and special will be returned threefold by her devotion and love.

Pisces with Pisces

Put two Fish together (indecisive creatures to begin with), and you'll find a relationship with lots of frustrations. It'll take forever to plan a Friday night out! What they *do* have in common is that both are romantic to the core. They love music, movies, and the latest gossip. Pisces live a soap-opera existence: no Pisces is without some sort of drama in his or her life. There's always a crisis or concern to overcome. A better choice for a Pisces is an earth sign—Taurus, Capricorn, or Virgo. However, Pisces can dream big dreams together and live in romantic escape.

♥ ♥ ♥ Attraction
♥ ♥ ♥ ♥ Compatibility
♥ ♥ ♥ ♥ Communication
♥ ♥ ♥ ♥ Friendship
♥ ♥ ♥ ♥ Marriage Material

How about Bow Wow and Jessica Biel?

Pisces with Aries

Aries may grow tired of Pisces' incessant whining, but loves the attention Pisces showers on him or her. As long as Pisces doesn't smother Aries, Aries will look down from his or her pedestal with appreciation. This relationship benefits Aries more than Pisces in the long run. The two can make a go of it if both parties share in the responsibilities a commitment brings. The flirty Ram makes the Fish feel insecure, so the Ram needs to tame the urge to be a tease.

♥ ♥ ♥ Attraction
♥ ♥ Compatibility
♥ ♥ Communication
♥ ♥ ♥ ♥ Friendship
♥ ♥ Marriage Material

Niki Taylor and Ewan McGregor?

Pisces with Taurus

Taureans need to watch their tempers around sensitive Pisces, whose feelings could easily get bruised, but overall, this match works. Taureans want a lot of attention and affection. Pisces could smother and mother them all they want! The Bulls will help bring Pisces back down to earth when they get caught up in their dream world. If they can't make a decision, logical Taurus will make it for them. Worries are lifted! Crown these two Prom King and Queen!

♥ ♥ ♥ ♥ Attraction
♥ ♥ ♥ ♥ Compatibility
♥ ♥ ♥ ♥ Communication
♥ ♥ ♥ ♥ Friendship
♥ ♥ ♥ ♥ ♥ Marriage Material

Jensen Ackles dating Kelly Clarkson?

Pisces with Gemini

A serious dating relationship between these two should not be taken too seriously. The Gemini would probably agree. If a Pisces falls head over heels in love, there's danger ahead! Gemini's fickle nature and need for variety will bring the Pisces great disappointment. The two could carry on brilliant conversations, their creative minds work well together, but Pisces won't be able to see through their rose-colored glasses that a commitment will not work. The Fish may hang on to the relationship long after Gemini has moved on.

♥ ♥ ♥ Attraction
♥ ♥ Compatibility
♥ ♥ Communication
♥ ♥ ♥ ♥ Friendship
♥ Marriage Material

What about Freddie Prinze, Jr. and Jewel?

Pisces with Cancer

This pair would be worth betting on. Pisces and Cancer tend to feel more deeply than some of the other signs. Cancers can get quite moody around the full moon. Pisces are like sponges—they soak up everything in their environment. If their moods are in harmony, then most of the time the relationship works. If there are lots of emotional ups and downs, there will be problems. They are naturally caring, sympathetic, and kind. If they bring these qualities out in one another, the union will prosper. This duo can be tres' romantique!

♥ ♥ ♥ ♥ Attraction
♥ ♥ ♥ ♥ ♥ Compatibility
♥ ♥ ♥ ♥ Communication
♥ ♥ ♥ ♥ Friendship
♥ ♥ ♥ ♥ ♥ Marriage Material

Could you imagine James Van Der Beek and Michelle Branch?

Pisces with Leo

Here's where Pisces can play their role very well. Pisces love to please and Leos love to be pleased, but it's a two-way street. Leos need to make sure they don't take Pisces for granted or they'll become cold fish. Most astrologers say this is not a match made in heaven. I agree, but I have seen cases that have worked out wonderfully. If there's mutual compassion and both parties benefit, I like the idea.

♥ ♥ ♥ Attraction
♥ ♥ Compatibility
♥ ♥ ♥ Communication
♥ ♥ ♥ ♥ Friendship
♥ ♥ ♥ Marriage Material

Can you see Brittany Daniel with Drew Lachey?

Pisces with Virgo

These opposites can easily make things work if they take the time to listen to one another. They actually make a pretty good team. Virgo will fuss over Pisces' clothes, hairstyle, and what the Pisces is ordering on his or her pizza. Pisces will just fuss. But these two love to be together, just hanging out at home, renting movies on the weekends, or studying for an exam. Virgos like to help people and Pisces like to please. Things won't always run smoothly, but they won't run from each other when the going gets tough. Both hate breakups.

♥ ♥ ♥ ♥ Attraction
♥ ♥ ♥ Compatibility
♥ ♥ ♥ ♥ Communication
♥ ♥ ♥ ♥ Friendship
♥ ♥ ♥ ♥ Marriage Material

Robert Iler and Fiona Apple, anyone?

Pisces with Libra

Since both have indecisive minds, these sun signs would probably drive each other nuts, but they hate to offend. Pisces likes to stir the pot every now and then. Libra hates confrontation. The upside to this union is that there'll be plenty of romance. Libra and Pisces love to be in love. But in the long run, the relationship could be frustrating and will probably wear thin.

♥ ♥ ♥ Attraction
♥ ♥ Compatibility
♥ ♥ Communication
♥ ♥ ♥ Friendship
♥ ♥ Marriage Material

Shaquille O'Neil and Serena Williams.

Pisces with Scorpio

Intense Scorpio may be too much for Pisces to handle over the long haul. The relationship has merit, though. Pisces indulge Scorpios with lots of hugs and kisses. A Pisces will also find a Scorpio to be a strong ally who is in his or her corner during times of crisis. Scorpio's natural healing powers can soothe Pisces' worries and emotional ups-and-downs. Since these two are water signs, they can tune in to each other's feelings. However, Scorpios need for privacy may make the smothering Fish feel neglected and rejected.

♥ ♥ ♥ ♥ Attraction
♥ ♥ ♥ ♥ Compatibility
♥ ♥ ♥ Communication
♥ ♥ ♥ ♥ Friendship
♥ ♥ ♥ ♥ ♥ Marriage Material

Freddie Prinze, Jr. and Kelly Osbourne.

Pisces with Sagittarius

This is one of those relationships in which gullible, trusting Pisces could get hurt. If the Sagittarius is mature, the relationship will be strained at times but can work. If the Sagittarius wants to date around, Pisces is likely to be disappointed. Spending too much time together doesn't work for this pair. Stay friends, and don't cross the love line!

♥ ♥ ♥ Attraction
♥ Compatibility
♥ ♥ ♥ Communication
♥ ♥ ♥ Friendship
♥ Marriage Material

Consider Dave Moffatt and Katie Holmes together?

Pisces with Capricorn

This nice blend of a water sign and an earth sign lends itself to long-lasting compatibility. Stoic Capricorns may not always understand Pisces' strong emotional nature, but this quality helps to soften their hearts a little. It's best if both have outside interests and friends to keep them happy so they don't get too dependent on one another. Mutual respect is a must for survival. Overall, these two should get along very well.

> ♥ ♥ ♥ ♥ Attraction
> ♥ ♥ ♥ Compatibility
> ♥ ♥ ♥ Communication
> ♥ ♥ ♥ ♥ Friendship
> ♥ ♥ ♥ ♥ ♥ Marriage Material

How about Drew Barrymore and Jim Carrey?

Pisces with Aquarius

Go ahead and meet for lunch, but I wouldn't agree to anything more than that. These two make better friends than steady dates. They could ruin a wonderful friendship if they step over the line. Aquarians need their space. Pisces may take this as rejection. As a business team, they'd do well. Pisces' creative abilities coupled with Aquarius' smarts could create a huge money-making venture, but romance is likely to be a letdown.

> ♥ ♥ ♥ Attraction
> ♥ ♥ Compatibility
> ♥ ♥ Communication
> ♥ ♥ ♥ ♥ Friendship
> ♥ ♥ Marriage Material

What about Taylor Hanson and Brandy together?

What a Pisces Is Looking for in Love

Pisces want someone who is a soul mate, someone with whom they feel a strong mystical connection. They want someone who can be very romantic and sensitive, and someone who will spend all of his or her free time with them. They're looking for a guy or girl who isn't afraid to talk about feelings, dreams, and a future together. Pisces love "psychic" stuff such as tarot cards, tea leaf readings, and astrology. They believe in magic and happily ever after. Create a storybook romance, and they'll never forget you!

First Date Ideas

Plan a day of swimming or just hanging out at the beach. A romantic movie is a good choice, too. Walks in the moonlight, a poetry reading, or dancing under the stars are ideas that would delight your Pisces. To the Fish, it really doesn't matter where you go or what you do, just as long as you are together!

The Dumped Pisces

When Pisces are dumped, they will "boo-hoo" for weeks. When you say good-bye, turn and run because Pisces will want to know what they ever did to cause you to lose interest. They want details! They'll call, write, and ask their friends to intervene on their behalf to win you back. Don't give them any indication that you'd ever consider getting back together, or they could turn into stalkers. Once they realize that this romantic fairy tale is over, they'll move on to another. Secretly, they may enjoy playing out this drama. Pisces do love a good soap opera!

How to Attract a Pisces

- Ask a Pisces for his or her help

- Compliment a Pisces on his or her amazing eyes

- Write him or her a mushy poem

- Give him or her a mischievous wink

- Show the Pisces your sensitive side

Never Ever

- Hurt a Pisces' feelings

- Ridicule a Pisces' dreams and ideas

- Forget that Pisces are psychic

- Take him or her for granted

- Use or take advantage of his or her kind nature

2

Burning Love

Would you like to draw a special love to you? Thousands of people all over the world have used candles to help create magic in their love lives. Growing up in a traditional Catholic family, whenever we had an urgent request, we'd go to church, light a candle, and say a prayer for our special intentions. I remember when I was nineteen years old and at college. I had just broken up with my boyfriend and went to the campus church before class to light candles and ask God to bring us back together. I still recall, as if it were yesterday, how many tears I shed. I'm one of those extra sensitive Cancers! I lit three candles near the altar: one for me, one for him, and one that represented both of us. I asked God for just one more chance for things to work out between us, and promised I wouldn't take his love for granted ever again. I felt so much better after that, and really believed with my heart that everything would work out. Shortly after saying the prayers and lighting the candles, we got back together! We were on again and off again for several years. But it seemed that every time I started lighting candles to get my boyfriend back, I'd hear from him.

Candle burning has been used since ancient times by people from all walks of life and religious beliefs to affirm their intentions and draw the "perfect love" to them. It should be stated that when you work with candle magic you are creating a special energy that you release into the universe. Any time you work with energy you are creating magic. Some people use this technique only for good. Others may use it for selfish or negative reasons. It is my belief that you should always work from the standpoint of using candle magic for your highest good and that of others.

Here is a unique story about a friend of mine who sent energy out into the universe. The universe responded to her, but not in the way she had hoped or imagined. Sarah was in an unhealthy relationship with her boyfriend Matt, who was really a jerk. He had two girlfriends on the side, lied to her, cheated on her, and made a lot of empty promises. They would often break up, but she took him back every time he called. No matter how abusive he was to her, Sarah believed Matt loved her and would eventually change.

After yet another difficult breakup and a confrontation with his other girlfriend, Matt left once again. Sarah didn't hear from him for weeks. She heard rumors that he had moved in with Girlfriend Number Three. This tenacious Cancerian gal wasn't about to give up. She knew he wouldn't return her phone calls, so she started burning pink candles every day. Pink candles are used to create more love in your life and draw a relationship to you. She did not know at the time that pink also helps create self-love, which was something Sarah needed after experiencing such a huge loss of self-esteem.

Sarah carved Matt's name and her own on a fresh candle every day. Like clockwork, at the same time each day she burned the candle and said a little affirmation for Matt and her to get back together. This went on for months, but Sarah never gave up. Then one day magic happened! A heavy snowstorm hit her city and she had to get to the grocery store. She kept putting off the short trip, but something kept telling her she'd better get to the market. As she pulled into the parking lot, a car pulled in right beside her. She glanced over at the driver. It was Matt! He was smiling at her. All flustered, Sarah got out of the car. To her disappointment it wasn't Matt, but this guy looked just like him! He was the same height, size, and sported the same blonde hair and twinkling blue eyes as Matt. The young man was immediately drawn to Sarah. Sarah was attracted to him, too, because he was a dead ringer for her ex. When the guy said "Hi, my name is Matthew," Sarah almost fainted.

The two are now married and have a son. The universe works in strange ways. The candles worked their magic, but not in the way Sarah had hoped. Sarah had been praying for the universe to send her a happy relationship with Matt; one filled with perfect love. She got what she asked for! The new Matt is a great guy, and very devoted. The intentions and energy she put out into the universe by burning candles drew to her a love her heart and soul needed. Her prayers were answered. Magic happened . . . for her highest good!

The coolest part of this true story is that Matt didn't even live near the market. He lived in a town forty miles away, but a friend convinced him to visit. Matt thought he was going to the market to pick up some soda. Little did he know at the time that he was meeting his future wife!

I have many clients who have practiced the art of candle burning to draw love to them. My friend Dee was madly in love with a guy from her past. Fifteen years went by before she met up with him again. She asked him to a local dance, where she and some friends would be on Friday night. He would not give her a straight answer because he already had a long-time girlfriend whom he was thinking about marrying. However, he was still very much attracted to Dee, and she knew it! Dee began lighting candles all week to help draw this cute Scorpio to her. On Friday morning he approached her and said he had been thinking about her all week. He would meet her at the dance!

She got all dressed up and waited for him to show. It was 10 p.m. and he was not there yet. It appeared this guy was not coming after all! But across the room, her eyes locked with another guy's. She felt immediate attraction. He was so drawn to Dee that he got up and asked her to dance. Dee was really into astrology, so she asked him what his sign was. He was a Scorpio! They fell in love almost instantly, and one month later they were making plans to get married. Dee never runs into her old flame and doesn't even care. Her candle magic worked, but not in the way she had originally planned. The universe must have thought it was for Dee's highest good to meet this other Scorpio and for the old flame's highest good to remain with his girlfriend.

Both of these stories could have ended differently. If Sarah and Dee had been working in a negative manner, trying to control or manipulative magic, sending out bad intentions toward the old Matt, the ex-flame, and their girlfriends, they would have probably gotten a negative response. Because they were praying for love in a positive and pure way, however, magically, two good guys appeared in their lives. Both girls found the love they had longed for.

If you wish for something bad to happen to someone, it is likely that the same thing will come back to hurt you. Thoughts, intentions, and curses are like boomerangs. That's why you should always create magic for your highest good and that of others. Whatever you put out comes back to you. Maybe not right away, but in time. This is the law of the universe.

It's not the candle that's creating magic. It's your pure thought, or rather your "energy." The candle is merely a tool to help put that intention out into the universe. The flicker of the flame helps you focus and produce more energy. Energy creates action, and finally, an effect or end result. There's no set time frame for magic to manifest. You may find yourself becoming very impatient while waiting for your wish to be granted. There is a time and place for everything. Just don't give up too soon. Don't get discouraged if things don't happen quickly.

If you continuously ask for something and you see no signs of getting any closer to your goal, it may be time to reexamine those intentions. Are you asking for something that is really not for your highest good? Do you really need it? Would your desire hurt someone? Is your aim realistic? Say you want to date a famous singer you've got a crush on, but he's unattainable. You don't work in the music industry, so the chances of meeting him are slim. You're not Britney Spears so you won't likely run into Justin Timberlake. I'm not saying major miracles don't happen. You just have to be realistic.

This is a little embarrassing for me . . . but I feel I should share a personal story with you. When I was fifteen years old I had this mad crush on a famous country singer. He had a string of number one hits and was extremely handsome. I bought all of his records, joined his fan club, and was determined to marry him one day. I know this sounds silly now, but back then it didn't. I would pray every night before I went to sleep, "Please let me marry me this guy." This went on for two years. I would light candles at home, at church, and on New Years' Eve, and send my pleas out into the universe to meet and marry my country crooner. I wouldn't call myself a groupie because I had never been to one of his concerts. He had never done a show in our little town. But I was his biggest fan. In the meantime, I got a part-time job as a reporter for our weekly newspaper and I began writing feature stories. I was so proud of myself because I even got an official "press pass" with my photo on it.

I remember one summer night after I had just turned seventeen. I was so frustrated about never meeting my idol that I got angry and made one last plea, "Please, if I can't marry him, then at least let me meet him, and kiss him!" I Immediately felt relieved, and for some reason, I never prayed again to marry this guy. Little did I know, by changing my request and bringing it down to reality, the energy of the universe would now work with me. I must have muttered the right words, because a few weeks later, it was announced on our local radio station that my dream guy was coming to our town to do two concerts! I couldn't believe my ears. Remember, I had a press pass, so I spoke with his agent and requested an interview, and was granted thirty minutes before the show to meet with Mr. Wonderful. You have no idea how happy I was! The universe had heard and granted my request. The candle magic worked! I boarded the tour bus and my heartthrob came out from the back. I was so thrilled. I conducted a short interview, and before I got off the bus, he kissed me. (Oh, yes, on the lips!) That was the best kiss I have ever had in my life. I'll never forget it.

I believe miracles and magic can happen. My wildest dream came true. It wasn't for my highest good that I marry my country singer, but I did have several other opportunities to interview him over the years when I worked as a magazine editor. I want you to know that anything is possible. Sometimes you may have to adjust what you ask for and how you ask for it, but dreams do come true. So, if you really like Justin Timberlake, just make sure you use the *right words* in your pleas to the universe!

Whether you realize it or not, you create magic everyday. The words you speak, the people you touch, the smiles you share, all the bits and pieces of life make magic moments. Life itself is magic. Know that you can create and manifest anything your heart desires if you take the proper action and your will, intent, and purpose is strong. Burning candles gives your thoughts more energy. Use this ancient practice for a pure purpose and good will come to you!

The rules for candle burning are simple. Buy a candle in a color for a specific intention. Begin your candle burning on the day of the week that's best suited to your intention.

When I was young, my family said nine-day novenas, so we would burn our candles for nine days in a row for about an hour each day. Many people who work with candles burn their candles for seven days. Since this is the most common practice we will use this example.

Setup is easy. Find a nice, quiet area. You should burn the candles at the same time every day, in the same room and for the same intention. You should use a fresh candle every day. Always ask your parents for permission before you burn a candle, and make sure you never leave it unattended. Place your candle in a clear crystal, metal, glass, or wood holder. Make sure it is secure.

Sarah always placed a rose quartz gemstone near the base of her candle while it burned. Rose quartz is known as the love stone, and the energy from that particular stone aided her intention. She also placed a photo of her and Matt near the candle, too. If you do this, make sure your photo is far enough away from the flame so it doesn't catch on fire!

I suggest you burn the candle for ten minutes each day. If you cannot stay with the candle that long, burn it for at least two minutes each day. As you light the candle, say your affirmation out loud. You can write your own affirmations and prayers, too, or use the ones I've included.

Candle Intentions

To Attract Love to You

Candle color: Pink

Day: Tuesday if you're a girl; Friday if you're a boy

Crystal: Rose quartz

Affirmation: "I draw perfect love to me. I'm filled with the power of love and attraction. I give thanks for love in my life."

To Bring Back a Boyfriend or Girlfriend

Candle color: Deep purple

Day: Friday

Crystal: Rose quartz or pink tourmaline

Affirmation: "Our relationship is back on track. *(Name)* and I are in love and happy."

To Have a Great Date

Candle color: Red

Day: Sunday

Crystal: Turquoise

Affirmation: "We're having a wonderful time together on this *(say aloud the actual day and time)*. *(Your name and his name)* are experiencing lots of joy and happiness!"

To Stop Gossip About You and Your Love Life

Candle color: Orange

Day: Monday

Crystal: Black tourmaline

Affirmation: "My world is full of peace and harmony. There is no room for gossip and lies, about me or my relationships. I will not allow negative thoughts or conversation near me."

For Self-Confidence in Love

Candle color: Red

Day: Sunday

Crystal: Bloodstone

Affirmation: "I am confident, self-assured, and special. People are attracted to me. I am loved and appreciated. There is no fear of rejection around me."

For Peace In Your Relationship

Candle Color: White

Day: Thursday

Crystal: Jade

Affirmation: "All is calm in our relationship. We are growing in love and light, and peace and harmony each day. The white light of protection surrounds my true love and me."

To Dispel a Negative Situation/Avoid a Breakup

Candle Color: White

Day: Monday

Crystal: Black tourmaline

Affirmation: "Our relationship is safe and protected. Any negative energy, people, or problems are fading away as I speak. There is peace and harmony all around me and my love."

To Keep a Loved One Safe

Candle color: Silver

Day: Monday

Crystal: Clear quartz

Affirmation: "(*Name of loved one*) is happy, safe, and sound. No harm comes to him (*her*). (*Name*) is protected and blessed."

To Keep An Ex-Boyfriend or Ex-Girlfriend from Bothering You

Candle color: Silver

Day: Sunday

Crystal: Quartz

Affirmation: "I am free from negative people and situations, and am especially free from (*name*). (*Name*) cannot bother me or cause me any worry. (*Name*) will forget his (*her*) feelings for me and move on."

To Overcome an Obsession with Someone You Can't Be With

Candle color: Yellow

Day: Tuesday

Crystal: Onyx

Affirmation: "I am strong in my convictions and free from this obsession. I will not allow myself to have deep emotional feelings for *(name)*. My will power is very strong, and I can conquer any negative desires."

To Release Anger After an Argument with a Boyfriend or Girlfriend

Candle color: Blue

Day: Thursday

Crystal: Pearl

Affirmation: "I immediately release any anger, hurt, and frustration I feel toward *(name)*. Our relationship is at peace once again."

To Forgive Someone

Candle color: Blue

Day: Thursday

Crystal: Chrysocolla

Affirmation: "I forgive *(name)* for the harm, pain, or hurt he *(she)* brought me. I let go of any resentment he *(she)* has caused me."

To Make the Right Choice Between Two Guys or Girls

Candle color: White

Day: Monday

Crystal: Peridot

Affirmation: "I am able to choose one love with confidence; the best choice for me is evident. I am filled with peace and happiness regarding my decision. Serenity and peace surround me with my choice."

To Overcome Fear to Ask Someone Out

Candle color: Gold

Day: Sunday

Crystal: Onyx

Affirmation: "I am free of any fear or anxiety. I release any worries. I am self-confident and assured that I am a good person. Anyone would love to have me for a friend and boyfriend (*girlfriend*). I feel great about myself!"

To Build Self-Confidence and Self-Esteem

Candle color: Red

Day: Sunday

Crystal: Citrine

Affirmation: "My self-confidence is growing. I know I am a wonderful, talented, bright, attractive person with so much to offer. I am proud of who I am and know I can conquer anything I set out to do. I am very powerful."

To Overcome a Difficult Situation in a Relationship

Candle color: Blue

Day: Thursday

Crystal: Blue lace agate

Affirmation: "I give thanks for being able to overcome difficulties and challenges in a positive way. Problems and obstacles fall by the wayside. My path is clear and inviting. No harm comes to me."

To Make the Right Decisions Regarding a Relationship

Candle color: Blue

Day: Thursday

Crystal: Calcite

Affirmation: "I give thanks for having the knowledge to make correct decisions now. I am open to receiving truth and support from the universe."

To Change Your Love Luck (And to Attract a Rich Guy or Girl)

Candle color: Green

Day: Friday

Crystal: Citrine

Affirmation: "I am lucky in love. I am fortunate to draw so many wonderful people to me. All good things come my way. Any negative energies leave me immediately, and my path is open to success."

For Protection Against People Trying to Break Up Your Current Relationship

Candle color: Black

Day: Saturday

Crystal: Black tourmaline

Affirmation: "We are safe and protected. No evil can come near me and *(name)*. We are strong and pure, secure in our relationship and love. No negativity can harm us, hinder us, or break us apart."

To Learn the Truth about a Matter Regarding a Relationship or Attraction

Candle color: White

Day: Monday

Crystal: Opal

Affirmation: "I can clearly see though my eyes correctly, hear through my ears, and understand the truth through my mind. No one can fool me. The truth has set me free!"

To Stop Jealousy

Candle color: Greenish yellow

Day: Sunday

Crystal: Quartz

Affirmation: "Gone are the negative people who are envious and jealous. I am not affected any longer by people who are consumed with jealousy."

To Find Your Soul Mate

Candle color: White, purple, and pink

Day: Thursday

Crystal: Amethyst, rose quartz, and clear quartz

Affirmation: "I am inviting my soul mate to come into my life now. I am ready to embrace you with an open heart, mind, and soul. I am thankful for your presence and love."

3

Romancing the Stone

Working with Gemstones to Bring Love into Your Life

In chapter 2 you read Sarah's story and know how she used rose quartz crystals (also known as the "love stone") to increase the love energy in her life. Many people believe that crystals have power. The gemstone jewelry that you wear attracts certain types of energy to you. Do you ever feel drawn to a piece of jewelry at a store? Do you always wear a certain ring or necklace? Do you feel "bare" without it? For thousands of years, people have been using crystals to help draw and create powers of healing, love, protection, and prosperity.

Gemstones and crystals are part of nature's abundant creation. Crystals hold unique energies. These energies draw or vibrate to different things. One of the nicest crystals you can find to increase your love vibration is the rose quartz stone. It is a soft pink color. The rose quartz helps heal broken hearts and promotes self-love too.

There are many other stones that can help get your love vibe working, but the rose quartz is the most popular. You can wear it or carry it in your pocket. You may not notice anything different right away, but after a while, people will seem extra friendly, and that crush you've had your eye on may stop by your locker and say hello. Some crystal lovers place the stone on a photograph of the person of interest to enhance the love vibration or keep a relationship strong to avoid a breakup.

When you choose a stone or crystal, I suggest you follow your intuition. Pick a stone you are drawn to. If a crystal warms up in your hand, the energy it possesses will work for you. If it stays cool to the touch, it's not going to work its wonders, so keep picking.

For years I have been attracted to pink tourmaline jewelry. Not pink ice or sapphire. Even the beautiful pink zirconia would not do. I was drawn to the pink tourmaline. It is not the easiest stone to find, so whenever I ran across a ring or necklace, I made sure to buy it. I felt something was missing if I didn't wear the stone or carry it with me. There are different colors of tourmaline, but the pink is a heart stone that strengthens creativity. It enhances your love vibration, too. At that time in my life I needed the energies the stone had to offer. I don't wear the tourmaline as much as I once did, but I often find myself reaching for it at least once a week.

Here's another personal story I'd like to share. A few years ago, I was going through a bad breakup. I bought a rose quartz heart-shaped pendant and wore it every day. I even slept with the necklace. After nine months of wearing the stone, my ex came back and wanted to work things out. On our first date, we made a pact to make our relationship work. The next morning I realized my rose quartz necklace was gone! It was nowhere to be found. I searched high and low for it. The clasp on the necklace was strong, so I knew it didn't break off. I came to the conclusion that the stone had served its purpose and vanished. Its mission was completed. It played a part in bringing love back into my life. Other people have shared similar experiences they have had with their love stones vanishing into thin air.

Love stones can also be used to create energy, to open up the heart chakras, and to help soothe your emotions. When you first buy a crystal, it is important that you cleanse it to make it yours. Sitting in a store all day, it probably absorbed everyone's energy, so you will want to release that as soon as you buy it and bring it home. I always place my crystals in saltwater overnight. Never let anyone wear your love stone unless you want to carry their energy or issues around with you! Here's a simple guide to enhance your love life through the power of specific crystals and stones.

To Attract love
- Rose quartz
- Ruby
- Pink calcite
- Pink tourmaline

To Let Go of Negativity and Release Problems in a Relationship
- Jade

To Increase Popularity with the Opposite Sex
- Barite
- Turquoise

To Get Rid of Butterflies in Your Stomach when He's Around
- Fluorite

To Boost Self-Confidence So You Can Ask Someone Out (Or Say "Hi!")
- Bloodstone
- Pyrite

To Ease Depression After a breakup
- Chrysocolla
- Aventurine
- Smoky quartz

To Keep Jealous People from Interfering in Your Love Life

• Black tourmaline

To Take Away the Jitters on a First Date

• Amber

• Blue lace agate

To Relieve Stress During a Love Crisis

• Onyx

• Pearl

• Blue topaz

To Heal a Broken Heart

• Emerald

For Meditation and Healing

• Quartz crystal

• Moonstone

Here's a List of Gemstones and Crystals, and Their Uses

Agate: Carry this stone with you when you're finding it hard to break a relationship off. When you don't want to hurt someone's feelings, this stone will make it easier to cut ties.

Alexandrite: If you can't get up the nerve to start a conversation or ask someone out, wear alexandrite. It will help calm the butterflies in your stomach.

Amber: If you've got a mad crush on someone and can't think, eat, or sleep because he's always on your mind, this stone will work wonders! It's known to soothe, and brings emotional balance to its wearer.

Amethyst: Anyone who wants to increase his or her psychic ability should wear this. You'll "tune in" to who your secret admirer really is!

Aquamarine: Reduces nervousness about someone you have a crush on. You'll be friendlier and less apt to put your foot in your mouth when your love interest is around.

Aventurine: Helps overcome shyness. Wear it and you'll feel optimistic and happy!

Bloodstone: If a shot of self-confidence is what you need to ask someone out, put a bloodstone in your backpack.

Barite: All of your relationships will run more smoothly with this stone.

Blue Lace Agate: Dumped for someone else? This stone will soothe emotions and pain.

Calcite (clear): Helps overcome any fears. Wear it and you'll see the truth clearly . . . you'll know the guy you like is for real or a real jerk!

Calcite (green): Releases fear. If you get tongue-tied around someone special, you'll find just the right words to say.

Calcite (pink): Helps let go of past hurts. Draws unconditional love to you. If you can't let go of an old love, this will help.

Carnelian: Carry this stone and you won't get all google-eyed when your crush sits beside you!

Celestite: You'll feel like talking up a storm with your latest love!

Chrysocolla: Balances emotions, reduces fear of rejection, and will help an upset stomach if you get nervous before a big date.

Diamond: Good healing stone. Intensifies the power of other stones.

Emerald: Works on all matters of the heart. When you're going through a breakup or are on the outs for a while, wear emerald to heal the heart.

Fluorite: Good for meditating to draw your true love to you!

Garnet: Inspires passion and love.

Gem Silica: This is a rare and beautiful stone. Helps girls unlock their feminine side and helps guys get in touch with their sensitive side.

Jade: Promotes universal love. Radiates divine, unconditional love. Dispels negativity.

Jasper: Powerful healing stone for the heart.

Kansas Pop Rock: Does your relationship need a boost? Is it boring? Grab a pop rock!

Kunzite: Used by many to overcome obsessions with an unrequited love. Heals heartbreak. Enhances self-esteem and acceptance.

Kyanite: Promotes truth, loyalty, and reliability in relationships.

Lapis: Brings old love wounds and emotional hurts to the surface for healing.

Moonstone: When there's trouble in your love life, the moonstone will work wonders. It relieves your heartache.

Onyx: Relieves stress after a fight with your honey.

Opal: Absorbs negative energy and creates peace between couples.

Pearl: Softens the pain of a heartbreak or a loss.

Pyrite: Promotes a positive outlook on your love life.

Quartz: The "everything" crystal. Magnifies the intensity of other crystals. Keeps negative energy away.

Rose Quartz: The love stone. Vibrates and draws love to you!

Ruby: Great love stone. Ruby promotes your zest and passion for life.

Sapphire (blue): Creates loyalty in love. If someone is after your sweetheart, your sweetheart will be true to only you!

Smoky Quartz: Good to fight depression and disappointment after a romantic disaster.

Tiger-eye: Softens stubbornness in a relationship. Helps one to see "both sides of the coin" in an argument.

Topaz (blue): Promotes tranquility and peace in a relationship that's rocky. It has a soothing effect on its wearer.

Tourmaline (pink): Heart/love stone.

Tourmaline (watermelon): The best heart healer.

Tourmaline (black): Offers protection from negative people who want to keep you and your true love apart.

Turquoise: Good friendship stone. Give to someone you care about.

4

The Color of Love

Did you know that wearing certain colors can make us feel cozy, happy, relaxed, or anxious? We can even go so far as to say that the colors we wear can draw certain reactions from others. Just as you might choose to wear a rose quartz necklace to create romantic energy around you, our clothing colors make a statement, too. We set our mood for the day in the morning when we pick a dress or shirt to wear to school. Obviously, if you want to create a love vibe, you'll want be very selective in the colors you choose. Here's a list of colors and what they mean.

Pink stands for love. If you choose to wear a pink shirt or dress, you can draw love easily to you. Romance is in the air. People around will find you very attractive. Wearing pink shows you are open to giving and receiving love.

Green is another good color to wear, but not necessarily the best for your love vibe. It's a healing color. People will feel warm and cozy when they're around you. If someone is down, he or she will feel much better after spending just a few minutes in your presence. You'll be approachable. Also, wear green if you're nursing a broken heart or need to balance your emotions.

Blue is a color of peace and understanding. It has a calming effect. People feel comfortable and relaxed around you. They feel drawn to your gentle nature. Blue helps you to relax. It's easy to open up to someone who is wearing blue.

Yellow is the color of communication. Wear it if you need the courage to ask someone out. If you're going on a date, it will help the conversation flow easily. You'll feel more creative and lighthearted. Those who wear yellow feel spontaneous and quick-witted. You'll know just what to say and how to say it. Your sense of humor shines. If asking for favors or talking over a problem in a relationship, wear yellow.

Purple is a spiritual color, and is considered lucky. You'll feel optimistic about love and life. If you wear purple, people see the good in you. A soul mate will easily be drawn to you on a purple day.

Red is the color of passion. It can be very sexy. It gives you energy and drive. Sometimes it is viewed as a powerful color, and wearing it at the wrong time can intimidate some people. Red is not good to wear if you are hoping for a certain person to ask you out. He or she may chicken out! But wear it if you want to grab someone's attention. It's red-hot, and will surely get you noticed!

Orange is the color of joy! It brings energy and happiness. A person wearing orange is exciting to be around and creates good energy. Wear orange if you're feeling down about a breakup or disappointed in love.

Gold makes you sparkle and feel like royalty. People love things that glitter and shine. Wear it when you want to be the center of attention. Grab the spotlight. Feel like a million bucks. You'll attract a lot of admiration from the opposite sex, too.

Gray is not a good color to wear unless it's mingled with other colors. It sends the message, "I am all business; I can't be bothered with love." Be sure not to wear gray if you're going through a breakup or are on the rebound. Gray can really drag you down emotionally.

White is a nice, clean color, and people will safe and secure with white. If you don't know what to wear, put on a white shirt. It's neutral and inviting.

Black is mysterious and dark. To some it says, "Stay away. I'm in mourning." To others it says, "I'm mysterious and intriguing." If you're looking for love, use it sparingly, except on a night out, when lots of black looks very classy.

And speaking of colors, most of us will either buy or receive colorful roses and flowers. They have special meaning, too. If you're a guy trying to get a special message to your leading lady, take notes. If you're a girl who's just received a single rose, there may be more meaning behind the gesture than you thought. Read on.

Flowers and Their Most Common Traditional Meanings

Red roses: I love you

Yellow roses: Friendship

Pink roses: I admire you; you're special!

White roses: Innocence; spiritual love

White/red roses: Unity

Orange roses: Desire

Lavender roses: Love at first sight!

Chrysanthemum: You're a wonderful friend

Carnation (solid): My answer is "Yes" to love

Carnation (striped): My answer is "No" to love

Daffodil: You are the only one

Hyacinth: I'm sorry

Black roses: It's over

5

Love in the Palm of the Hand

Love Lines

Do you know that the lines in your palms reveal how lucky you'll be in love? For thousands of years, people all over the world have been seeking out palm readers for advice about the tiny markings and network of lines that reveal true love and heartache.

When you are looking for romance or just flirting with a real cutie, you probably notice the person's eyes first. Sometimes it's the smile that we're drawn to. But if you really want to get a clear picture of someone's personality, you should look at his or her hands. Isn't that a little difficult to do? Sometimes, but not always. You can tell a lot about someone's personality just by shaking his or her hand. If you're wondering whether the object of your affection is a soul mate or just a fading fancy, take a closer look at his or her hand shape. It can reveal more than you can imagine.

There are four types of hand shapes, and each one of them relates to one of the four elements in astrology, which are air, earth, water, and fire. Let's look at each shape and discover more about its meaning.

The Air Hand

This hand usually sports a square palm with a lot of fine lines. Long fingers indicate that these teens are creative, curious, and love to talk and express themselves. The air hand people are usually emotionally stable. They love to make new friends and help people. Think of these people as helping hands. Many air hands dream of being teachers, journalists, writers, and social workers when they get older. In love, they are looking for mates and dates who are fun to be with, have a good sense of humor, and possess a positive attitude. They get bored with the same old routine, so if you are interested in an air hand, make sure you're open to trying anything once!

Because the air element relates to Gemini, Libra, and Aquarius, many people born under these zodiac signs have air hand qualities.

The Air Hand

The Earth Hand

These teens have a square palm with short fingers and deep lines. Earth hands are more serious-minded and practical types. They like sports, physical activities, and appreciate nature and the outdoors. In relationships, the earth hand likes to take things slowly and see how things progress before he or she falls in love. Some earth hand people are cautious and take a long time to let you know they're interested in you. They're hard to catch but easy to keep. Once they make a commitment, the earth hands will stick with you through thick and thin. They are looking for love with someone who is down to earth and easygoing. These types appreciate long-term relationships and don't need to date a lot of people at once. It takes a lot for them to end a relationship, but once they do, it's for good. They usually don't go back once they say goodbye. The Earth Hand is associated with Taurus, Virgo, and Capricorn people. If you were not born under any of those signs, you may still possess some of the earth hand qualities.

The Earth Hand

The Water Hand

You'll recognize a water hand because of its rectangular palm and long fingers. These guys and girls are very sensitive and emotional; they love from the very depths of their souls. Some are shy and quiet. Others are outgoing and very creative. Both have wonderful imaginations. In love, they are looking for commitment and romance; a knight in shining armor or a princess to rescue. They believe in living "happily ever after" and "until death do us part." Make no mistake about it, water hands fall head over heels in love. Sometimes they tend to smother a partner because they desperately need security in love, so they should hook up with the steady earth hands rather than the changeable air hands or fire hands. The water hand is associated with the zodiac's water signs of Cancer, Scorpio, and Pisces, who share their traits.

The Water Hand

The Fire Hand

Look for short fingers on a rectangular palm that boasts clear-cut, definite lines. Fire hands are found on people with a high burn rate; meaning that these teens have lots of energy and are always on the go. Fire hand people possess lots of charm and charisma. They love a good challenge. Always ready for action, fire hands fall head over heels in love. Many are creative. Some enjoy competitive sports. These folks are fun to be with! There is never a dull moment. They love to travel to exciting places, are considered thrill seekers, and are always first in line to ride a roller coaster. In relationships, they want to share lots of affection, romance, and fun with their boyfriend or girlfriend. Fire hands relate to the fire signs Aries, Leo, and Sagittarius.

The Fire Hand

Check It Out!

When you're checking out the hand of a guy or girl you've got a mad crush on, there are a few things to consider:

1. The thumb

2. The shape of the finger tips

3. The fingernails

4. The thumb placement and flexibility

5. The length of the fingers in relation to the palm

Tom Thumb Reveals All!

Someone got you all confused? Can't seem to put your finger on it? Look at the thumb! It can help you determine someone's true personality. Look at the:

1. Length

2. Placement

3. Flexibility

The thumb will reveal clues about a person's ego, drive, and sex appeal. It can give clues to someone's personality, especially whether or not someone is stubborn or strong-willed. Thumbs also show weaknesses and energy levels.

Take a closer look:

Short Thumb: Shows a lack of self-confidence. This person may have problems completing projects and usually cannot stay in a relationship for a long time. Generally, a person with a short thumb has love trouble because he or she gets bored easily. One of my best friends from high school has a very short thumb. She was married and divorced five times by the time she was thirty years old.

Long Thumb: If your thumb reaches past the joint of the index finger, you have a lot of physical drive and energy. You can be very sexy, but also quite bossy. Many long thumb types thrive on being the center of attention. Members of the opposite sex may find these teens very attractive.

Low-set Thumb: These people are fiercely independent and able to think quickly on their feet. They're fun and spontaneous. In relationships, they won't settle for less than their heart's desire. They love being in love and the thrill of a new romance.

High-set Thumb: These people can be tense and rigid with affection. They are very cautious in love, and play mind games. Sometimes people with high-set thumbs are very insecure or may have been hurt in past relationships. They have a tendency to withhold emotions so they won't get rejected.

The Tip of the Thumb: This is also another important aspect to look at. If it bends back easily at the first joint, the person is flexible and easygoing. He or she can adapt to almost any situation. This guy or girl is a winner, and makes for a great love match because of his or her generous heart and affectionate nature.

Warning! If the tip of the thumb bends back too easily and is extremely flexible, don't get too close! This one could be a cheater and schemer . . . likely to play the field!

A thumb that is moderately flexible means you possess plain old common sense. You can be quite stubborn, however, and are unlikely to budge if you strongly believe in something. Once you set your mind to something, there's no turning back.

Stiff Thumbs: These are the folks who resist change and have lots of trouble saying, "I'm sorry," or even meeting you halfway during a disagreement. They can be very stingy with affection, too. You will feel as if you're doing all of the work to keep the relationship alive. If there's a breakup, they won't give in and will expect you to come crawling back! On the upside, stiff thumbs can be reliable and stable.

Are you intrigued? Wanna learn even more? Oh, yes, there's so much more that I can tell you, so much more to share about how the hands, fingers, thumbs, and even fingernails can reveal a lover's personality and disposition.

Fingertips

There are four types of fingertips you'll want to memorize. The tips of the fingers will reveal even more interesting info on your potential love interest.

The Cone Fingertip: Visualize a finger that tapers off to a delicate point. This is called the "cone." If you have your eye on someone with a cone fingertip, he or she is very sensitive. Consider this person to be romantic, as cones "live to love."

Cones are also intuitive. They react to their environment and can "pick up" easily if you are interested in them. You won't have to drop many hints if you find them attractive; they already feel your vibes!

The Round Fingertip: These friends are just plain fun! They are relaxed, easygoing types who despise mind games and power plays. They go with the flow. Many are excellent communicators and love to talk, swap stories, and share ideas. Just don't tell them your biggest secret, because they like to blab! They wouldn't intentionally expose a confidence, but may kiss and tell. Their heads and hearts are equally balanced, so these teens are ideal if you want a good, stable relationship.

The Square Fingertip: You'll find longevity in love here. Square tippers usually hang on and hang in there. These folks are confident, self-assured, and like themselves . . . sometimes a little too much. Egos can get in their way, but overall, these people are salt of the earth types and once they make a commitment, they will honor it. They'll except the same from you. No flirting with anyone else allowed!

The Spatula Fingertip: These fingertips flare to a very wide tip and belong to free spirits who love adventure. They're hard to tie down, but when they do make a commitment, it's serious business. Spatula people are the best bet for long-term romance. Seldom do they stray. If you are open minded and not the jealous or smothering type, the spatula could be a match for you.

Nail 'em Down!

Nails

Whether you paint them bright pink or purple, or leave them au natural, your fingernails can tell a great deal about your character. In order to truly get a good "read" of someone's nails, it's important to view the bare nail with no polish. Here's a closer look at daggers!

Long Broad Nails: If someone has nails that are slightly rounded, he or she will have psychic abilities. These teens will be ethical, open minded, and fair. They'll want to take a relationship slowly and really get to know you before moving into a steady dating commitment.

Long Narrow Nails: Sometimes people with these claws are selfish, manipulative, and egotistical. They don't trust anyone and will make you jump through hoops to prove your love. If you're the one with long narrow nails, don't be alarmed. You may not have these tendencies, but be forewarned that you could develop them.

Short Nails: There's no consistency with a short-nailed lover. If short nails are not due to the bad habit of biting them, they reveal a person who may not stick around for very long. They jump from one relationship to the next, and are often negative and depressing to hang out with.

Jagged Nails: These nails indicate that there will be many highs and lows in your love life. The good times are really great, but the breakups can be devastating. People with jagged nails fall in love hard and fast, but seldom do their relationships last. How they respond and handle their crazy love lives says a lot about them. They love and lose, but seldom do they give up. If you're a jagged nail, try not to wear your heart on your sleeve. But don't give up on finding true love, either!

Large and Broad Nails: You are physically fit and competitive by nature. These teens need to be on the go all the time, and can be quite charming. They usually have a string of admirers and plenty of dates. They are hard to tie down, but a lot of fun. There is never a dull moment.

Nail Color

Did you know that a person's natural nail color can determine how sexy he or she is? Read on!

Reddish color: This person is passionate, but a reddish tint near the bed of the nail also signifies a bad temper.

Pink: A loving, kind person who is very romantic, affectionate, and nice to be around.

Blush: A person with a cool and aloof attitude. Sometimes these people have a hard time dealing with the depths of feelings, and can't express how they really feel.

Pale: This nail hue indicates emotional blockages and problems. These people may not be as lucky in love as their friends, or may be unable to draw people to them easily. Shy.

The Love Lines of the Palm

Think of your palm as a road map of your life, a guide to romance and love. When reading the palm you should always read your dominant hand, the one you use the most. Therefore, if you are right handed, read the right hand. If you're a lefty, read the left hand. On another note, the lines in your palms can change from month to month and year to year, depending on the emotions, the crises, the fortune, and the paths you experience. A palm reading done in August may not be the same as a reading done in December. Examine your palms every so often. You'll be amazed at the changes you may find.

If you're like millions of other teens who want to see what their love line (a.k.a. the heart line) has to say, it will be extremely important to look at your palms every few weeks to see if there are any changes in this line. It will tell you when a new love interest is coming your way or if a breakup will occur. This is the line of the palm we'll explore in depth.

In order to get a good palm reading, you should have a magnifying glass so you can pick up the smaller, faint lines in the hands as well as the more defined ones. The deeper the line, the more strength its meaning will have. Faint or shallow lines show a lack of strength and energy. The number of lines is also a key factor. When you look closely at your palm you will see many lines; some long, others short and faint. These lines, along with meshing, netting, crosses, and other designs, are called palm markings. For a few specific definitions, read on.

Palm Markings

Branch: A line branching off from the original line. It usually means a change or new direction in a relationship. Perhaps a new love is on the horizon. If you're already dating someone, you could break the relationship off now.

Crosses: Two lines that are intersecting on a line means a struggle or hard times. The event or problem will be one you will not likely forget. Expect a crisis in your love life soon.

Stars: Seeing stars means your dreams will come true. Stars mostly show up on the head or heart lines. Expect true love to come to you!

Triangles: A good sign. These tell of happy times ahead in romance.

Breaks: Breaks mean endings. If there is a break in your heart line, it could mean the end of a relationship. If the broken line begins in a new direction, it means a complete change and a new love interest.

Netting or mesh: Usually shows up in your palms when you're tired and overwhelmed by your love life, and nothing seems to be going right in matters of the heart.

The Heart Line

The Heart Line is the most important line in your palm to foretell of love and romance. Think of it as your emotion barometer, revealing your sensitivity, capacity to love, and the amount of love and attraction in your life.

Your Heart Line is the very top line on your palm. It starts a bit below your little finger and runs across the palm.

Let's interpret your Heart Line:

- Small branches that swing upward from the Heart Line mean you will have a happy love life and lots of good friends. The more upward branches you have, the more popular you will be.

- Branches in a downward position mean heartbreak or disappointment in love and friendships.

- If your Heart Line curves up, you fall in love fast. You wear your heart on your sleeve and can get hurt easily. But you rebound quickly and are soon off to capture more hearts! Romance is very important to you. You are a passionate person. The bigger the curve, the more romantic you are!

- If the Heart Line is straight or has a small curve, you are cautious and not as apt to fall head over heels in love. You are loyal and will make a great husband or wife. You're a little too logical at times, and will need to make an extra effort to give hugs and kisses.

- Long, straight Heart Lines mean that you are very intense, jealous, and possessive. You give 110 percent in a relationship, but can be a little controlling.

- If your Heart Line turns down at the end, it means that you can be moody and hard to deal with. You won't find this example much. Most Heart Lines curve upward, but if you're dating someone whose Heart Line turns down, you can expect the relationship to be stormy! If you have such a line, you may want to change some of your attitudes about love and be more optimistic.

On a sheet of paper, write down some things you have discovered about your Heart Line.

The Heart Line

The Fate Line

The Fate Line is also known as the Destiny Line. This is not one of the major lines in the palm, but when I am looking for answers regarding romance, I also look at the Fate Line. Some palmists call this the karma line. It runs from the bottom of your hand through the middle. It first and foremost will show what you are supposed to do with your life—its true purpose and path. Secondly, it can foretell what a future husband or wife will do for a vocation. In addition, it reveals what is important to you in life; what your values are. This information will help you determine how successful a relationship can be. If a guy you like has a similar line, then it's a safe bet that he'll be a good date. If your lines are mismatched, the relationship may not work as well because you have different objectives and goals.

Let's examine your Fate Line more closely:

- If the Fate Line on your dominant hand is well defined, you are an independent person. You don't want a bossy or possessive mate who will smother you or hold you back from achieving your dreams.

- If the Fate Line runs up the middle of your palm to your index (pointer) finger, you will be very ambitious in your career. You'd make a good business person, lawyer, or police officer. A career will be of utmost importance to you, so you will need to make sure you don't neglect your personal life. You could put off marriage in order to build a career.

- If the Fate Line moves straight up to the middle finger, you are a born leader. You would be good in politics, business, and supervising, managing, or teaching others. You need a partner who will allow you to take charge and not try to deter you from your goals.

- A Fate Line that falls under one of your ring fingers shows that you are dramatic and creative. You'd make a great actor, musician, or artist. You will be sentimental and romantic when it comes to love, or you could marry a rock star or someone who is in the public eye!

- If your Fate Line leans toward your little finger, journalism, writing, broadcasting, and teaching are some careers to consider. You need someone who will communicate. If you end up dating someone who doesn't express himself or herself, the relationship may not last long.

- If your Fate Line starts in the middle of your palm, expect to become successful a little later in life. It may take a decade or longer to decide what it is you want to do. That's okay, as everyone matures at a different level. You may be well into your thirties when you feel you are ready for a serious relationship. You could value freedom more than commitment.

- If the Fate Line starts at the bottom of the palm and ends midway up, you'll start working at a young age and retire early. You may decide to marry and have kids earlier than some of your peers. When it comes to love, you may be very mature.

- If your Fate Line doesn't start until it reaches the Heart Line, your love life will always be more important to you than work. Your world will center around those you love. Strive for more of a balance between your career and your partner.

- If the Fate Line is deep, this means you are determined to succeed. Nothing will stand in the way of your goals. You will leave a relationship if need be to become a big star or further your career ambitions.

- If the Fate Line comes to an abrupt end at the Heart Line it means you have emotional barriers that keep you from finding lasting love. Some of you may have a problem with commitment, and others may have built up walls because of past heartache. You don't want to get hurt again, so you protect yourself.

- If there are a lot of breaks, there may be difficulties and career losses. Breaks also mean many different types of employment. You could bounce from one job to another, or your spouse could!

- A long line that runs from the very bottom of the hand to the base of the fingers is the sign of the workaholic. If you have this type of line, be sure you learn to balance work and play. You'll never get a chance to meet someone if you're stuck at work all day!

- A Fate Line that ends in a fork means you may have to make a big decision or that there will be a career change at some point in your life. That decision or change could have a major impact on a relationship.

- A star at the bottom of the Fate Line means you will find success and happiness in your chosen career.

- For those who have no Fate Line, it merely means that no set path has been made. You will create your own.

On a sheet of paper, write down what you have learned about your Fate Line.

The Fate Line

The Marriage Lines

Marriage Lines are short, horizontal lines under your pinky finger that go almost to the edge of the palm. The lines that go up and down and through the marriage lines are called your Children Lines. They represent how many kids you're likely to have. You will need a magnifying glass to read these. The Marriage Lines can tell you how many trips down the aisle you'll make and other interesting things about committed relationships. Even your past relationships are etched on your palm. Did you know that new lines appear just before a new attraction waltzes into your life? And those same lines disappear just before the relationship comes to an end.

Let's interpret the Marriage Lines:

- Short, feathered lines mean short relationships that go nowhere. Longer, deeper lines mean that steadier relationships are in your future.

- A single deep line stands for long-term commitment or one marriage.

- Two deep lines equal two long-term marriages.

- If you have several lines you can expect a lot of relationships and commitments. Usually the number of lines represents the number of marriages. If the Marriage Line ends in a fork, that marriage will end in divorce.

On a sheet of paper, write down what you have learned about your Marriage Lines.

The Marriage Lines

Of Special Love Interest

There are two other areas of interest you should examine when reading the palm for love indicators. First, there is a line that complements the Heart Line and indicates long-lasting relationships or ill-fated ones. This line is called the Girdle of Venus. The Mount of Venus is found at the base of your thumb. Look for its specific markings to determine even more secrets about your love life.

The Girdle of Venus

This can be one line that turns upward and looks like a crescent moon. It usually stretches from the middle finger to the ring finger, or it can be made up of two lines, one under the other. If you have this palm marking, your emotions run deep. You sympathize with other people. However, this can lead to problems. You could get depressed worrying about everyone else's sorrows! Don't get so wrapped up in a relationship that you can't think of anything else! Don't become obsessed with a guy or girl. If you have this marking it is important to stay away from negative influences. You are apt to be drawn to the bad boys or fickle girls who love to play mind games. On the upside, if you find someone wonderful, you'll truly love him or her from the depths of your soul!

The Girdle of Venus

The Mount of Venus

Mounts are fleshy mounds in different areas of the palm. There are many of these mounds, but the one we are going to be concerned with is the Mount of Venus. Look at the diagram below to find where the Mount of Venus is located. Now, find yours. You will notice that your Mount of Venus has lines or markings on it, such as crosses, squares, or maybe stars. These markings give you a better idea of your love traits. You may need a magnifying glass to see all of the markings.

Let's interpret the Mount of Venus Lines.

A Flat and Hard Mount: You've had your heart broken a time or two, and have probably been disappointed in love in the recent past. You could be afraid of rejection and getting hurt, but you should try to break this pattern to invite new love into your life.

Lines: If you have two or more lines you may not have consistent relationships. You could feel like breakups are your fault or that your boyfriend or girlfriend never appreciates you. But you do have hope that the right one will come along!

Strong lines: These lines suggest that you have a very strong influence on members of the opposite sex. You could be charismatic and popular!

Mixed Lines: You are passionate and powerful. People feel you have it all and are drawn to you easily. However, shy people may feel a little intimidated around you. Make them feel more at ease.

Islands: These indicate a person who feels guilty a lot. "If only I did this or that, he would love me more," is something you may say if you have islands.

St. Andrew's Cross: One true love! A large cross is a sign that you will find your soul mate! A small cross foretells a happy love affair.

Star: A star near the thumb means a wonderful, blessed, and joy-filled marriage that will likely last a lifetime, but if the star is at the base of the mount, it foretells heartbreak with members of the opposite sex.

Square at the Base of the Mount: If you have this marking you need to get out of the house and make it a point to find true love. Otherwise, you might live a sheltered life and meet no one.

Triangle: If you have a triangle mark you may be manipulative and marry for money over love. You sometimes use people for your own advantage and have a tendency to be quite selfish.

Grille: You have a very romantic nature. You are gentle, kind, and affectionate!

The Mount of Venus

The Handshake

We've covered a lot so far, but to grasp the entire picture of someone's love personality, you really must read the whole hand. Besides the markings and the lines, the fingertips, and the nails, you must take into consideration the entire hand. When it comes to making certain distinctions, touch is very important. One of the best ways to get to know someone is to shake hands with him or her. Here are a few pointers:

- If a person thinks he or she is better than you, that person will merely shake your fingertips.

- If a person's shake is weak, it means a relationship will not develop into anything serious.

- A strong, firm, and long handshake signifies someone who really wants to get to know you better and is interested!

What About the Hand Itself?

A soft, flat hand with a big indentation in the center of the palm means that the person is needy and smothering. He or she can drain your energy. This person could use you, and is unable to form deep commitments.

A thin, hard hand represents a stubborn person. It's a good bet that this person will be inflexible, cheap, and insensitive.

A thick, fleshy hand belongs to someone who's sexy, has a high energy drive, and is warm and affectionate. This person loves to be in love.

A hand of medium thickness shows a strong capacity to live life to the fullest and to love deeply.

A thick hand that is cool to the touch means that the person is aloof and afraid to get too close. He or she is more intellectual than emotional, and has a hard time trusting people and warming up to others.

Summing it Up

A perfect love hand is not easy to find, so if someone has more pluses than minuses, yet some undesirable lines, don't dismiss the relationship. Here are a few of the best things you can find when looking for love in the palm of the hand:

- Strong, defined Heart Line with little or no breaks

- A pinkish nail color

- A firm but flexible thumb

- Straight, slightly curved fingernails

Here are a few warning signs of "bad love" hands:

- A bluish or pale nail color

- Twisted fingers

- Lines that are weak

- Many unfavorable breaks or markings in the Heart Line

- Stiff, inflexible thumb

Know that every hand likely has good and not so good characteristics, just as people have good and bad habits. If you find someone has a lot of negative markings, it's probably not best to pursue a relationship with him or her.

Most of our relationships begin with a simple handshake. Learning even just a little bit about the hand and palm lines can save a lot of time and heartache when you're searching for someone to love.

6

Love Numbers

You've got the palms down, but there's another key to unlocking romance that is easy to use, too. So simple, in fact, that all you need to do is add numbers together! This next theory is called Numerology (the study of numbers and their meanings).

A person's birthday reveals more than you can imagine about his or her personality, and numerology can help determine compatibility between you and another person in a matter of seconds!

Numerology can also help you identify your ideal love match. It's as old as the ancient science of astrology. Just as we have an astrological sign, we also have a birth number. It can help you discover hidden talents, positive and negative traits, and can even foretell the future. In this chapter I'll take you through three different formulas that will:

1. Reveal your birth number (personality)

2. Find your love number (love/soul mate number), which will identify compatibility with the guys or girls you like

3. Predict the next nine years of your love life (using my own special formula)

How To Determine Your Birth Number

The process is simple. First, write out the day, month, and year in which you were born. For example, if you were born on October 12, 1985, you would write down the number like this: 10/12/1985.

Then add together the numbers in three separate parts (month, date, and year). For example:

Month 1 + 0 = 1

Day 1 + 2 = 3

Year 1 + 9 + 8 = 5 = 23

Now add the three totals together:

1 + 3 + 23 = 27

You want to reduce the final number down to a single digit of 9 or less:

27 is 2 + 7 = 9

So the birth number for someone born on October 12, 1985, is the number 9.

Birth Numbers

Now read the following pages to learn more about your birth number and its personality traits.

 Number One

Famous Ones: Eminem, Halle Berry, and Charlize Theron

Number One teens are confident leaders. They are independent types and like to live life in the fast lane. Most number Ones are very competitive. They want to be adored and loved by everyone. In their teen years, Ones enjoy hanging out with adults rather than kids their own age. They are more mature than most of their peers. They think they can "have it all" and will do their best to get ahead in life. Many times they do. If you're a One, you have a lot of enthusiasm for life. In your heart, you know you are special and deserve great things, and you work hard to get them. Don't be critical and impatient with others who may not see things your way. You can be mature for your years, but you don't know everything. . . just not yet!

When dating, Ones like to show off their partners to their friends. They prefer dating the most popular athlete or the smartest girl in class. Ones brag about how many girls are calling them or how many guys have asked them to Homecoming. At times, Ones can be competitive in love. If they have their eye on you, better watch out, because they won't stop pursuing a relationship until you agree to a first date. Ones are fun and exciting to be around. There's never a dull moment!

Positive Number One Traits

- Confident

- Talented

- Passionate

- Emotional

- Craves success

- Ambitious

- Smart

Negative Number One Traits

- Big ego

- Self-centered

- Obsessive

- Overconfident

- Narrow vision

- Materialistic

- Selfish

Number Two

Famous Twos: Madonna, Bill Clinton, and Gwen Stefani

Number Twos are compassionate, lovable, and huggable! Twos draw many unique people and friends into their lives. Their main life lesson is love. They learn and benefit when working with partners and groups. Twos have easygoing personalities and strive for peace and harmony in their love lives. Friendships, family, and other loved ones will be their focus. Many of these relationships have a fated quality about them; perhaps these people are brought together to deal with past life issues. Many Twos meet and marry their soul mates. However, some Twos find relationships troubling; either they can't meet the "right one" or they have a problem settling down, even though they desperately want to. This is just part of the lesson they are here to learn. Romance is very important to a Two. Girls often fantasize about their wedding day years before it happens. Guys long to be the knight in shining armor for their princesses. Both sexes believe in the theory of soul mates. If a Two is dateless or single for long, he or she feels empty. It's really important for them to be in a steady relationship. Their love lives are sometimes more important than good grades in school. They can't go to the prom without a date—that would be unthinkable! When dating, they are joined at the hip with the object of their affections. Because Twos get so caught up in love, they can neglect their friends. If your friend is a Two and currently single, don't count on your relationship staying the same when your friend falls in love. Twos really don't mean to dismiss you, it's just that love consumes them. But when there's a breakup (and there eventually will be), guess whose shoulder they'll want to cry on? If you are a Two, it's important to balance all of your relationships, including friends and crushes. Love is grand, but don't miss out on all of the other wonderful things your teenage years have to offer!

Positive Number Two Traits

- Friendly

- Good hearted

- Easygoing

- Faithful

- Calm

- Compassionate

Negative Number Two Traits

- Too sensitive

- Secretive

- Stubborn

- Possessive

- Revengeful

- Neglectful

 Number Three

Famous Threes: Cameron Diaz, Reese Witherspoon, and Drew Barrymore

Threes are wonderful communicators. They are creative and imaginative. Many make excellent teachers, writers, and artists. Most possess a good sense of humor. Their masterminds are always ticking. However, some Threes can be too cautious and don't take enough chances. It's important that they don't allow fear to deny them experiences that will enrich their lives. Threes place a big emphasis on friendships. They date in groups. The social scene is important, and they love just hanging out with their best buds. In love, Threes can be a bit fickle if they're not really serious about you. They like variety and change, but once they make a commitment, it's usually solid. Threes want a boyfriend or girlfriend who will really listen to them. They need to be able to share their deepest feelings. Born with a gift of gab, these teens can burn up the phone lines! They enjoy good gossip and are known to be blabbermouths. Threes are good-hearted people, though. They usually keep friends for life.

The only thing that stops Threes from finding love is their fear of rejection, so it may take them some time to muster up the courage to talk to you or ask you out. You may have to be the first to break the ice and say hello!

Positive Number Three Traits

- Generous

- Sensitive

- Excellent communicator

- Romantic

- Cheerful

- Social

Negative Number Three Traits

- Insecure

- Fickle

- Superficial

- Gossipy

- Inconstant

- Spends money frivolously

Number Four

Famous Fours: Demi Moore, Arnold Schwarzenegger, Avril Lavigne, and Will Smith

If you're a number Four, you are dependable, trustworthy, and probably more mature than your friends. You like to help others but need to be appreciated for these efforts. Your family is important to you. Fours are serious about their studies and do well in school. Some Fours need an extra push to go out into the world. They want to succeed and often do, but home is hard to leave. If you're a Four, the first semester of college dorm life may be difficult if you're far from mom and dad. You never forget a best bud's birthday, your parent's anniversary, and to call grandma. Heirlooms, genealogy, and the family tree are things you hold dear. A sense of belonging to something is important, whether it be your school's soccer team or the student council. You sense other people's pain and feel deep empathy. Because of these nurturing qualities, Fours make great doctors, nurses, counselors, and teachers. Fours need to feel as if they fit in and "belong," and usually try hard to please people. They want everyone to like them so they may go overboard to win approval. In relationships, they like to date one person at a time, and a relationship can last all the way from high school through college. Some marry their childhood sweethearts. Fours need to take more risks and go after love. If you're a Four, don't worry about rejection. You won't meet new people unless you make it a point to get out of the house. Take a chance on love. Your boyfriend or girlfriend will know he or she can depend on you through thick and thin. You expect loyalty, honesty, and lots of love from him or her because that's what you intend to give your honey, too!

Positive Four Traits

- Loyal

- Conservative

- Practical

- Romantic

- Supportive

- Traditional

Negative Four Traits

- Too serious

- Reserved

- Stubborn

- Cynical

- Rigid

- Strict

Number Five

Famous Fives: Beyoncé Knowles, Kelly Osbourne, Paul Walker, and Abraham Lincoln

Fives are creative and fun! They usually have lots of goals that they want to achieve. Some are into music and art. Others enjoy creative writing, theater, and poetry. Fives get bored easily and hate feeling confined. In romance, Fives enjoy the chase more than the capture. They like working toward the goal rather than reaching it. Fives can easily date more than one person at a time and are known to play the field. They flirt shamelessly! Fives don't always need to be in a relationship, either. They feel comfortable in their own company and are known to go without a boyfriend or girlfriend for years. Fives are hard to tie down for long! Change is important to them. If their lives get dull or complacent, they'll look for new mountains to climb or they'll throw a big party! And speaking of parties, Fives throw the best bashes. Because they are spontaneous, anything can happen. If you have a friend who is a Five, you will find him or her great fun, but unpredictable. There's never a dull moment. Fives win popularity contests. Seldom do people talk badly about them, except for their jilted boyfriends and girlfriends! Lucky in love, they could break a few hearts along the way. Fives don't mean to hurt anyone, they just look at life as one big party.

Positive Number Five Traits

- Curious

- Optimistic

- Adventurous

- Creative

- Gifted

- Lucky

Negative Number Five Traits

- Inconsistent

- Reckless

- Fickle

- Restless

- Erratic

- Superficial

6. Number Six

Famous Sixes: Ben Affleck, Justin Timberlake, Anna Paquin, and Stevie Wonder

If you're a number Six, you may want life to be organized and run like clockwork. You're apt to be a very deep thinker. Most Sixes have their lives all planned out early on. They know what they want to do when they get older. Many find jobs while in their teen years and are honest, dependable workers. Sixes have their fair share of luck, and then some.

Most Sixes are considered cool, attractive, and very charming. Often they take on leadership roles like class president and team captain. Peers look up to them a lot, so they run the risk of having inflated egos. However, Sixes are mostly down-to-earth. In their teen years, they learn to multitask and can fit a great deal into their hectic lives.

In relationships, Sixes are not mushy romantics. They are polite, reserved, and respectful. Appearances matter. They feel that the people they date reflect themselves. Often they wish to date the best-looking guy or the most popular girl in class. What others of think of them matters, but not nearly as much as what they think of themselves. They safeguard their reputation, so dating drama queens is something they avoid.

Positive Number Six Traits

- Loving
- Resourceful
- Realistic
- Fair
- Charismatic
- Sympathetic

Negative Number Six Traits

- Crafty

- Shallow

- Tense

- Manipulative

- Egotistical

- Inhibited

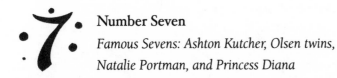

Number Seven

Famous Sevens: Ashton Kutcher, Olsen twins, Natalie Portman, and Princess Diana

Number Sevens are nice to everyone. They try to make everyone feel comfortable and at ease. They have a great sense of humor. Sevens are very romantic and make great boyfriend or girlfriend material, but stand in line, because they have their share of admirers. They are honest with their feelings but do not like to fight or argue. Sometimes they'll avoid confrontations, but when a love affair turns sour, they'll fight to keep it alive.

They daydream a lot, and can get lost in romantic movies and sad love songs easily. Sevens find new age and the occult interesting, too, as they tend to look at the world from a spiritual perspective. They're always searching for answers . . . and their soul mates. Because of their charm, Sevens seem to know everyone in town. They have lots of friends in and out of school and, surprisingly, of all ages. They may have an old boyfriend or girlfriend on one side of the tracks, another one west of town, and yet another smack dab in your own neighborhood! There's sure to be lots of gossip going around concerning a Seven and his or her love life!

Positive Number Seven Traits

- Wise

- Spiritual

- Honest

- Generous

- Romantic

- Sympathetic

Negative Number Seven Traits

- Boring

- Overly sensitive

- Withdrawn

- Scheming

- Isolated

- Stuffy

 ### Number Eight

Famous Number Eights: Josh Hartnett, Matt Damon, and Missy Elliot

Consider yourself lucky if you're an Eight. You always land on your feet and can draw money and special favors easily. At the very least, you'll be showered with beautiful gifts and a great clothing allowance. Many Eights become affluent and quite successful in life. However, they should learn that money isn't everything. You're always thinking about how to get another buck or trying to convince mom you need an extra twenty. Some people call you a hustler; others will say you're aggressive and a go-getter. You know one day you'll be super rich! Status symbols and nice clothes are important. Designer labels are a must. Even though you're not always into the latest fads, fitting in is important. Not all Eights are materialistic. They just like money because it allows them to do more things and buy more clothes! They enjoy treating their friends. Eights are generous people and love giving as much as receiving.

When it comes to love, Eights can be overly generous. They enjoy buying cards and little presents for their sweeties. When they fall for someone, they fall hard and fast. They'll do whatever it takes to make a relationship work. Their hearts are sometimes even bigger than their wallets! Eights will try to impress the object of their affections with their money or the cars they drive. If you fall for an Eight, you'll be treated to the finest things life has to offer . . . if not right away, then someday. Eights have great potential to make the most out of life and love!

Positive Number Eight Traits

- Practical

- Honest

- Fair

- Powerful

- High achiever

- Successful

Negative Number Eight Traits

- Misunderstood

- Stubborn

- Self-centered

- Demanding

- Jealous

- Ruthless

:9: Number Nine

Famous Nines: Kirsten Dunst, and Mahatma Gandhi

Number Nine is the most powerful number because it contains all of the other numbers' qualities. Nines have lots of energy. They can't sit still! They love having a full plate of things to do and a weekend crammed with activities. They don't plan and plot a lot—they take action. Strong-willed people, Nines are restless souls and quite impulsive. They have quick tempers, but most of the time they are happy-go-lucky. Nines always seem to get their way, and that's because they never give up. They are accused of being spoiled brats. It's not their fault! In their defense, everyone gives in to them. Not too many people can say "no" to their angelic faces and sweet smiles.

If a Nine has his or her heart set on you, watch out! Nothing will stand in his or her way of this love conquest. However, Nines tend to be a bit selfish and expect their partners to say "I'm sorry" first after an argument, even if the fight was their fault! Yes, they are frustrating but oh, so lovable. Nines should wait until they are in their late twenties or early thirties to settle down. Their wanderlust is tamed by then, so they're more apt to stay in a permanent commitment. But before that, anything goes. They fall in and out of love, depending on their moods. They're a lot of fun, and at times seem a little unapproachable to shy guys and girls, but once they flash their gorgeous smiles your way, there's no turning back!

Positive Number Nine Traits

- Emotional

- Enthusiastic

- Affectionate

- Bold

- Emotional

- Strong

Negative Number Nine Traits

- Restless
- Impatient
- Aggressive
- Conceited
- Insecure
- Vulnerable

Now that you've got the lowdown on your birth number, you'll also want to find the birth number for that guy you're madly attracted to or that girl you can't resist. Use the same method you did to find your birth number, except, of course, use the other person's birth date info. Be sure to reduce the number down to a single digit. Go ahead and read about his or her personality now.

Want to find out if you and your guy or girl are truly compatible, or if you are destined to be together? You may learn that the guy you like will be nothing more than a friend, or that he'll turn out to be real jerk! Or maybe this will be a soul mate match! To learn more you'll need to discover the love number.

The Love Number

To get this magic love number, add your birth number to his or her birth number. Here's an example:

Jack's birth number is 3

Jill's birth number is 7

3 + 7 = 10

Always reduce the love number down to a single digit: 10 = 1 + 0 = 1. So, Jack and Jill's love number is 1. Do you have yours ready? Read on for CCC (Couple Compatibility Combinations).

Love Number One

Number One Couple Compatibility Combinations:

1 + 9

2 + 8

3 + 7

4 + 6

5 + 5

Overall Impression

You stick together through thick and thin, but you'll likely have heated arguments. There'll even be jealous people who will interfere with your relationship. But stick together. Dream big. Support one another's goals and don't end a date mad. Always kiss and make up! Be sure to make time for outside interests other than the relationship, or it could grow stale. Sometimes too much of a good thing is, well, just plain too much!

Couple Compatibility Combinations

1 + 9: Don't follow anyone's rules for dating. Make up your own set as you go along. Number One needs to be more giving and learn from Nine about letting things roll off his or her back. Number One can be quite bossy and dominate the relationship, but Nine is not about to back down. Both of you are independent, bold, and high achievers. This can be a very good match, and one that can last a lifetime. The commitment you share will inspire both of you to reach for the stars!

2 + 8: This combination suggests a long-term romance, but only if Eight doesn't hurt Two's feelings! Two is *so* sensitive. Eight is honest and blunt, so a middle ground needs to be reached. Eight needs the stability and emotional nurturing that Two can provide. Two will "baby" the Eight. Eight will push Two out into the world and encourage him or her to fulfill his or her dreams. At times

this relationship will seem as if it's going nowhere. It may grow stale, yet neither party really wants to break up. Don't allow it to get boring.

3 + 7: Threes don't always want to see the truth. They want to trust everyone and can be naive. Whereas Sevens are not afraid to see both sides of a coin. Threes are dreamy and romantic. Sevens analyze things to death. This combination is 50/50. There are so many differences between these two numbers, but remember, "opposites attract." The relationship won't be boring, that's for sure!

4 + 6: Sixes need to feel thoroughly loved by another. Emotional security is really important. Home and family is very dear to them. They cry at the drop of a hat. Being too sensitive could be their downfall. Fours, on the other hand, are very logical and practical when it comes to love. They are traditional, honest, and believe in dating one person at a time. Generally, Sixes are not cheaters. Even though this combo is like yin and yang, Four and Six create a balance in one another's life.

5 + 5: There's never a dull moment when these two get together! Sparks fly and this couple could rush into things quickly. The biggest challenge in making this love connection work is finding common goals and interests. Fives are fun and always on the run! They dream big and have lots of things they hope to accomplish. One party will need to curb a tendency to be selfish and want his or her way all the time.

Love Number Two

Number Two Couple Compatibility Combinations:

1 + 1

2 + 9

3 + 8

4 + 7

5 + 6

Overall Impression

Compromise is the key in a number Two commitment. Talking things over and being honest with feelings is important. There's lots of chemistry in many of the number Two combinations. So, if your number falls in one of the paragraphs listed below, you're extra lucky when it comes to love. Don't take anything for granted, and appreciate the love you share! Many of your friends will think of you and your guy as the perfect couple.

1 + 1: When you are both working on the same goals and share the same ideals, this relationship is a piece of cake. Everything seems too good to be true. But if a nasty argument breaks out, watch out! You are like old war horses, stubborn and refusing to budge from your position. No one wants to give up the "power," and that's when this relationship could find its breaking point. Usually a 1+ 1 combination is best for friendships. If you want more, there could be tests and challenges that aren't easy to fix unless you're willing to bend.

2 + 9: You'll instinctively know the first time you meet that you're supposed to be together forever! This is a soul mate connection. The chemistry between the Two and the Nine is hot! Just make sure you don't keep secrets or play mind games, since both parties tend to be a little insecure. This combo can work because both like to party and have a good time. Two is a people pleaser and Nine doesn't mind being on the receiving end one bit!

3 + 8: This couple loves to party! There are a lot of shared interests. They feel like kindred spirits. You two can talk about anything until the wee hours of the morning. This is one of the best true love matches ever. Three and Eight are very attractive people and boy do they love to flirt! However, they are loyal. The biggest problem for this couple is finding time to cram all of their activities into one weekend!

4 + 7: Fours are practical and Sevens are analytical. Seem kinda dull? Not so. Sevens secretly long for a soul mate connection. There's an ethereal side buried deep below their safely guarded smiles. However, Fours care more

about how their significant other looks in a pair of low-rise blue jeans than the spiritual vibe they share. But all in all, this could be a relationship full of romance—something out of a dime-store novel if they let down their fences. There aren't many problems or cat fights here. This couple only needs to remember to work together as a team.

5 + 6: These two love to talk! They are drawn together easily, but may have to meet one another halfway in order for this love affair to last. Sixes feel as if they are doing all of the work to keep the relationship alive, while Fives take things day by day. As Sixes are planning for the future, Fives live in the moment. Sixes want commitment with a happy ending. Fives crave freedom. Do you see the writing on the wall?

Love Number Three

Number Three Couple Compatibility Combination:

1 + 2

3 + 9

5 + 7

4 + 8

6 + 6

Overall Impression

You both love to shop 'til you drop. Spending money as fast as you make it could be dangerous, but hey, it's fun! Life is a constant flurry of activity and drama. The number Three combo has lots of friends and won't tire of going to new places and meeting new people. This relationship will never be boring, but you'll probably be broke and owe mom and dad forever!

1 + 2: Number Ones like to get their way and tend to have a selfish streak. Number Twos are always trying to keep the peace, and they believe in compromise. Ones need to be more sensitive to their partners' needs if this relationship is

going to last. It's important to keep dating fresh and fun. Write little notes. E-mail him a love poem. Buy her a teddy bear. Surprise one another every day so boredom doesn't set in.

3 + 9: Three should think seriously before he or she utters the words "I love you" to number Nine. Nines will take what you say very seriously. They bet their life on love. So if you're a Three, choose your words very carefully. Some Nines have a habit of drawing all of the bad boys or the fickle girls. They want commitment, and most of their partners just want to flirt. Nines want to marry young. Threes choose to stay single for a while. As you can see, this relationship doesn't hold much hope.

4 + 8: This can work! Fours are grounded people, but they tend to be a bit cautious. Eights think things through as well. Neither number will wear their hearts on their sleeves. You must earn their trust. Eights like to be in charge, but they can play fair when it comes to the game of love. This couple plans their engagement, wedding, and honeymoon before their friends accept prom dates. Four and Eight is definitely a good choice.

5 + 7: Either they are too much alike or have absolutely nothing in common. Fives and Sevens will fall head over heels for one another, but will it last? Fives need constant change. They live life to the fullest. They hate feeling bored. Sevens must keep things interesting. There's a lot of chemistry here, but the sparks could fizzle out if dates get dull.

6 + 6: Loyalty is a big issue with Sixes. Never lie or cheat or you'll regret it! Since Sixes are honest and true to those they love, this combination leads to a long-lasting commitment. If someone ever wanted to cause trouble and break you two apart, he or she would have a hard time. This couple will stick together like glue. You have the same basic values regarding life, family, and friends. Life together is grand!

Love Number Four

Number Four Couple Compatibility Combinations:

1 + 3

2 + 2

5 + 8

4 + 9

6 + 7

Overall Impression

This is a combination in which opposites attract. The couple is different as night and day, but they don't care because they feel such a strong connection to one another. City slicker meets country bumpkin. New York City meets Des Moines, Iowa. Get the picture? Fours in general, however, are traditional types, so that's something you have in common.

1 + 3: Number Ones love adventure, so they're always coming up with exciting plans and ideas. Threes are ready for fun! They're diehard romantics, too. Ones aren't into all of that mushy stuff. This is not the best combination for love, but for casual dating and an interesting friendship, Ones and Threes are a perfect match!

2 + 2: You two are a lot alike and crave peace and harmony. In fact, you may never fight. Being on the same wavelength helps. Twos feel a strong need to put down roots together. You love being in love and making a relationship all that it can be. This couple can create magical moments together.

4 + 9: This is a great relationship if you need a study buddy or a co-chairman for the school dance. There's mutual support and respect. If one person needs help, the other comes quickly to help. Whenever there's a problem, you can depend on each other and get through it. When it comes to romance, however, it may take some time for an attraction to develop. It may or may not happen.

5 + 8: Since Fives crave change and Eights prefer more structure and security in their lives, this makes for a strange combo. Eights think a lot about how they can make an extra buck. Money is important to them. Fives couldn't care less if they spend their last dime, and they often do. Eights plan weeks in advance for a date, while Fives may cancel at the last minute. Fives throw caution to the wind. They hate to be fenced in, and are afraid of missing out on exciting adventures. The basic nature of each number is vastly different. This couple will work hard to make this relationship last.

6 + 7: You can't stand being apart, but if you're together too much you'll drive each other downright crazy! Traditional Sixes expect loyalty and commitment. Sevens don't kiss and tell, but they can lock lips with more than one person at a time. Sly Sevens are known to date around. They can't help it because flirting is so much fun! If the relationship lasts more than six months, chances are good that they'll be dating for a while.

Love Number Five

Number Five Couple Compatibility Combinations:

1 + 4

2 + 3

5 + 9

6 + 8

7 + 7

Overall Impression

Fun! Fun! Fun! That's the best way to describe this relationship. Expect to discover lots of new interests, hobbies, and friends. You certainly will not be bored. As long as you both keep the relationship exciting and fresh, this could last a lifetime. If it does end at some point, you will fondly remember this love as one of the best you've ever had, possibly the love of your life!

1 + 4: This combination is certainly worth a try, but there will be challenges because Fours want stability and long-term commitments while Ones like to keep their options open. That doesn't mean that Ones are two timers. They're just not in a rush to settle down with one person. Building a strong friendship foundation is a must if this attraction is going to last.

2 + 3: Twos can be shy, but Threes can draw them out of their shells. Threes love to talk and can keep a conversation going for hours on end. This relationship will be fun for a few weeks. It may fizzle out if Twos hide their feelings. Twos like time alone with their boyfriends or girlfriends. Threes have lots of friends who make many demands on their time. Get the picture?

5 + 9: Love at first sight! You two could move mountains together. Nothing seems impossible. Here you'll find mutual respect and admiration, but competitiveness as well. Be careful that you don't try to outdo each other. This isn't a competition to determine who's the top dog. It's a relationship—one that can grow to great heights if you become each other's cheerleader rather than opponent!

6 + 8: Love can last forever with this couple. Sixes and Eights both believe in true love and long-term relationships. Six adores Eight, and in turn Eight showers his or her beloved with lots of affection, attention, and gifts. This couple will manage to work through most any problem they encounter. However, if one person cheats, this relationship stands no chance.

7 + 7: Sevens are private people. Even your closest friends don't know all of your secrets. But put two Sevens together, and they're like kindred spirits. They understand one another and feel at home in this relationship. There's a lot of chemistry and a sincere friendship, too. It can blossom into wonderful love and devotion that grows deeper over time.

Love Number Six

Number Six Couple Compatibility Combination:

1 + 5

2 + 4

3 + 3

6 + 9

7 + 8

Overall Impression

A Number Six relationship is to be taken very seriously. There is no room for dishonesty, lies, or manipulation. If you enjoy your first date, then a second is made right away, and if that goes well, consider yourself on your way to a committed relationship! Long-term promises are made and high school sweethearts often head to the altar. This can be a steady, secure type of relationship.

1 + 5: Restless Fives won't get bored easily with adventurous Ones. Both of you have creative minds and enjoy going places. While this relationship doesn't last as long as many of the other Six combos (both partners like to play the field), this pair will have a lot of fun together! Many times these two break up only to reunite a few years down the road, after they've matured and dated around.

2 + 4: Cautious Twos may discourage Fours, who are ready to fall head over heels in love at first sight. It's not that Twos dislike Fours—Fours just may seem a bit mushy or overanxious to them. How can someone pledge undying love on a first date? If Four feels it, he or she says it. Twos are hard to catch but worth the chase. They'll give Fours the security they seek. Patience is the key to what could be a long-lasting love.

3 + 3: You're too much alike in some ways. If you feel more like family than boyfriend and girlfriend, then don't push the issue of a relationship. Just enjoy the friendship. You two have lots to talk about, and can probably read

one another's minds and finish sentences. There may not be a lot of chemistry, but there's sure a lot of camaraderie.

6 + 9: If Sixes don't smother Nines too much, this combination can be magical. Dramatic Nine loves to be adored and put on a pedestal. Sixes will give Nines all of the applause and admiration they can handle. The key to making this relationship last long is compromise. When these two really put their minds together along with their hearts, they will unlock a deep, soul mate connection.

7 + 8: Beware of the green-eyed monster. The downfall of this relationship could be plain 'ol jealousy. Eights want control. Sevens can be insecure if they don't get the attention they need. Seven is always overanalyzing what the Eight says and what he or she really means. If you don't sweat the small stuff, life and love become much easier.

Love Number Seven

Number Seven Couple Compatibility Combinations:

    1 + 6

    2 + 5

    3 + 4

    7 + 9

    8 + 8

Overall Impression

Is it destiny? True love? There is a fated quality to a Seven relationship. The first time your eyes meet, you immediately know this is not your ordinary connection, but something much more. Friends call you the "perfect couple." You feel safe, protected, and understood. This is your first true love, and one you'll never, ever forget. It has such a strong impact on how you look at your relationships and yourself for years to come.

1 + 6: It is very important to keep the lines of communication open. If you don't, there'll be misunderstandings and wrong impressions that escalate into major blowups. This couple has a strong desire to stay together, and there's no lack of physical attraction, either. However, Sixes feel they are always the ones to extend the olive branch if there's a fight. Ones need to be a little more giving, and Sixes need to speak up more often to get emotional needs met.

2 + 5: If you enjoy a real challenge, then take a look at this combination. You two bring out the best and the worst in each other. Fives don't like to be tied down, but Twos need to be in order to feel truly loved. While Fives love flirting with everyone at a party, Twos want time alone with their "special someone." If this couple can embrace their differences, the relationship flourishes. If not, it fades into a mere memory.

3 + 4: Three and Four complement one another. Both enjoy the same interests. Four helps bring Three back down to earth when he or she gets a far-fetched idea. Three teaches Four to dream big and chase after his or her wildest hopes and wishes. Both have a great sense of humor that keeps things lively, too. Your families expect you two to get married one day. Make sure to spend enough private time together to enhance such a good thing.

7 + 9: You'll feel as if you've met the guy or girl of your dreams if these are your numbers. This is a very spiritual connection, and there's a specific reason you are together. It may be that you're to help each other during a difficult time or be a source of encouragement. This is one of the closest combos and can lead to unconditional love. If it does not last, this relationship will be one you'll never forget or regret.

8 + 8: Watch out for power plays and don't keep score! There's a competitive edge to this relationship that could lead to all-out war. You're together . . . then apart. The constant breakup and makeup is driving you nuts. If you two really want to make this relationship work, then don't be so bossy! Make a point to speak up, but also say you're sorry when appropriate. You could be a dynamite duo, a real success story, if you keep egos in check.

Love Number Eight

Number Eight Couple Compatibility Combinations:

    1 + 7

    2 + 6

    3 + 5

    4 + 4

    8 + 9

Overall Impression

You are attracted to each other's intellectual side. You've met your match and feel as if no one has ever understood you until now! When an Eight relationship is formed, an excitement about life develops. You feel as if you're walking on cloud nine and the world is grand. Nothing is impossible and you dare to dream big! Don't screw this one up! Be mature enough to work out problems rather than run from them.

1 + 7: A fun fling, but it doesn't lead to a long-term thing unless you recognize the spiritual connection you two share. There'll be a mad attraction, but after a few weeks the momentum seems to dwindle. Keep the friendship alive if you can. Often it's the Ones who find they are longing for the Sevens if a relationships ends.

2 + 6: Sometimes Sixes consider Twos to be naggers. But Twos only want to help. Often their "advice" is taken the wrong way. However, both numbers are good listeners and will give each other a chance to be heard. They disagree on little things, but look at the overall picture the same. This is not a match made in heaven. It's good enough for now, but maybe not for forever.

3 + 5: Patience is the key to making this relationship last. You two may not understand each other very well. It takes longer to make up than to break up. Friends and family keep shaking their heads, taking bets on how long this relationship will last. You can fool them! Compromise, understanding, and forgiveness are the keys to unlocking an amazing love.

4 + 4: This relationship gets better as time goes on. You can count on one another when the going gets tough. Dependable, honest, and traditional in terms of dating and commitment, Fours like to date one person and have been known to stay in the same relationship for years—throughout high school and even college. You two can grow up together. Just make sure you don't take this relationship for granted.

8 + 9: These two share a karmic link, a past-life bond of some sort that initially draws them together. In some cases, this relationship only lasts until a specific lesson is learned or a karmic debt is repaid. However, it's not always easy to figure out what the couple is supposed to be learning. In time, these secrets are revealed, usually years after the relationship has ended and the two mature.

Love Number Nine

Number Nine Couple Compatibility Combinations:

1 + 8

2 + 7

3 + 6

4 + 5

9 + 9

Overall Impression

Couples involved in a number Nine relationship will tell you there was an immediate connection when they first met. The first meeting was not a coincidence but may have occurred under strange circumstances. The spark between a Nine couple cannot be ignored. There's such a strong connection between them. If this couple can recognize how special the bond is, this relationship will be the best they're ever had.

1 + 8: Love takes time to grow here because it must be nurtured. Trust could be an issue between this couple. Consistency is the key to making this a long-lasting union. There is a spiritual reason you are drawn to one another; how-

ever, past-life secrets will only be revealed after a period of ups and downs. If these two work out their differences, they'll see their love grow so strong that nothing can break it apart.

2 + 7: Two and Seven feel a connection, but they don't feel the same way about a relationship. Twos want to cuddle all the time and Sevens need space. This pair will have plenty of disagreements over silly little things. It's not the perfect match, but you could do worse. Try listening to what it is your boyfriend or girlfriend is telling you rather than anticipating how he or she should feel. Your perception of things will be quite different, so either accept that or end the relationship and look elsewhere.

3 + 6: Don't send mixed messages! Sixes don't feel secure about Three's flirtatious nature, but there's more to work on than just a jealous bone. Be open and honest with your feelings. Don't be afraid to express your opinions, but be sure to listen to one another's ideas, too. This relationship isn't always easy but somehow Three and Six always manage to find their way back together after a breakup.

4 + 5: Fours expect Fives to be around for the long haul. Fives hate to be in "love prison." However, this couple has staying power if they respect each other's differences. There'll be silly arguments over what's expected of each other. Friends could influence how you view this relationship, too, meaning that it's likely your best buds will despise your partner. Some are jealous of the fact you have such a good guy or girl. On the other hand, they may see things you're not seeing clearly.

9 + 9: You'll instantly be drawn to one another. You'll feel as if you've met a soul mate. For Nines, love doesn't always come easily, but this type of connection can last forever, especially if you cut one another some slack. Be there through the tough times and celebrate the good ones. This will be a rock-solid relationship if you're willing and ready to give it a try.

Maria Shaw's Predictive Numerology: How to Predict the Next Nine Years of Your Love Life!

You've discovered your birth number and the personality traits that go along with it. You've got your CCC number, too! Let's move on to the next love lesson in this chapter: predicting the next nine years of your love life! This is a simple formula that's easy to learn. You'll have no trouble finding your lucky love years and figuring out when you'll meet Prince Charming or an old toad!

In this numerology formula, your life runs in a nine-year cycle. Each cycle has a different love theme. You'll deal with different relationship issues each year. The cycles run from your birthday to your next birthday rather than calendar year to calendar year. Let's go over the formula you'll need to learn to find which love cycle you're in right now!

Love Cycle Number for the Year

First Step: Take your birth month and add it to your day of birth (do *not* include the year). For example: June 4 is 6 + 4 = 10. This is the tricky part: add the previous number to the current year master number.

To get your current master year number, take the year and reduce it down to a single digit. For example: 2005 is 2 + 0 + 0 + 5 = 7. Always reduce any number higher than 9 down to a single digit. For example: 10 = 1 + 0 = 1.

Following is a list of some master numbers:

2005: 7
2006: 8
2007: 9
2008: 1
2009: 2
2010: 3
2011: 4
2012: 5
2013: 6
2014: 7

Now let's go back and review our first step again. If your birthday is June 4 and the current year is 2005, then: June 4 is 6 + 4 = 10.

Now add 10 to the master number: 10 + 7 (2005 master number) = 17. Reduce 17 to a single digit: 1 + 7 = 8. The love number for June 4 in 2005 beginning on that birthday is 8.

It is extremely important to remember that this numerology does not run calendar year to calendar year. It runs from your birthday to your next birthday. For example, if your next birthday falls on December 31, 2005, you cannot use the master year number for 2005 until you reach your birthday. You will still be working off 2004's master year number until the end of 2005. If your birthday is April 1, 2005, you will be working off the 2004 master year number for the first four months of the calendar year. In April, begin using the 2005 master number.

Now that you have your Love Cycle, let's get on to predicting the next nine years of romance for you!

Number One Love Year

This year is filled with bright, beautiful beginnings. If you are single and ready for romance, now is the time to go after your heart's desire. Whenever you are in a number One love year, you will find true love and happiness, but you need to make the first move. Prince Charming isn't going to land in your lap, and, likewise, the girl of dreams will not drop from the sky. In other words, a great love life isn't being handed to you on a silver platter. You have to take action. Get out and meet more people. Look for love in all the right places. Attend school dances. Go to varsity sports games. Throw a party for all of the underclassmen. Any lonely heart coming into a number One year should take the time to create a wish list. This is most effective when done on your actual birthday. The list should include everything you want in a wonderful boyfriend or girlfriend. List everything. It doesn't matter if some of the things sound silly or superficial. Just write them down. This is *your* best love year. A friend of mine who has a birthday in June put "a new boyfriend" at the top of her list one year, and by October, she was going out with a great guy!

Be sure to be specific. If you write, "I want to meet a cute guy who is tall, dark, and handsome," he could be drop-dead gorgeous but have a huge ego. Be sure to put "not conceited," or "humble" on that list somewhere, too!

Number Two Love Year

The Two cycle is all about relationships. It's not necessarily a romantic time. It's more apt to be a time when you know exactly what you're looking for in a relationship (and what you have to offer someone else). If all of your friends are dating, you may want to find a steady guy, too. If you feel like a third wheel at times, don't get mad . . . get even! Get out of the house and make a point to meet new people. Smile at the cute guy whose locker is next to yours or say hello to the girl who cuts in front of you in the lunch line. This is not the year to be shy. The power of the Two love year lies in the energy that attracts new people to you easily. Thoughts are like boomerangs. If you think, "I'm going to meet someone," then you will meet someone! You're ready for romance. Did you know that many teens discover their first love during the number Two love year?

Number Three Love Year

As we move away from the Two year and into the number Three year, you may find yourself more social and outgoing than ever before. It's easy to meet new people now, and if you're looking for love, it'll be easy to find . . . maybe even in your own neighborhood. Since number Three rules friendships, neighbors, and travel, expect to meet a new love interest through your circle of friends. If you're taking a trip, you could meet a handsome stranger and begin a long-distance relationship. Your best bud may fix you up on a blind date. Go for it! School is another great place to make a love match. In fact, anything you're involved in that includes groups of people will benefit you. With your social life in full swing, you'll be attending lots of parties so make sure to always look your very best. New and long lasting friendships could develop, too. A close friend of the opposite sex may have a mad crush on you this year and finally have the nerve to reveal his or her true feelings!

Number Four Love Year

You're going to be so busy this year. It's hard to make time for a "main squeeze" (or even find one now), but if you want to make the honor roll at school or get a job, it'll be a piece of cake. Your social life takes a back seat. Often, your love life will be dull or you'll be too busy working to notice. You won't have as much time to spend with friends. You could land a job and have to balance sports, homework, and a weekend paycheck. If you still have enough energy left to date, where are you going to meet the guy of your dreams? Plain and simple: at work or at school. Since you'll be beating a path back and forth between the two, it's only logical that you'll meet someone there. Look for work at a place where you'll also have a chance to socialize a bit. You won't want to take a job babysitting. Opt for a job at the mall or pick up a hostess gig at a restaurant. There you'll come into contact with lots of people your age. You can also volunteer to tutor other students after school. Make sure you offer your services to your classmates only. If you're a senior girl, it's unlikely that you'll want to take a freshman to the prom!

Number Five Love Year

Count your blessings! This is the year to fall madly in love! It's the biggest time in the nine-year cycle to meet someone special. You may have more than one option. There'll be many admirers to choose from. It seems as if everyone's interested in you. Some of you may move or enroll in a new school during a Five year cycle, so keep your eyes open for those new "friends" who want to show you around town. If you're a guy, you'll make a big effort to get girls to notice you. That effort pays off when your phone begins ringing off the hook! If you're going out with someone now, watch out—someone new could steal your heart away!

Number Six Love Year

The number Six cycle is a time when you get down to business! You're really serious about life and grow up fast! If there's something you want to change, this is the year you'll do it. Many people kick bad habits in their Six cycle. If you want to end a bad relationship but didn't have the heart to do so in the past, you have the guts to break it off now. If you don't feel confident with yourself because of your looks or weight, you will lose a few pounds or change your entire style—a complete makeover! Changes are often good and can improve your chances of attracting new people. Where do you meet a new love interest? Maybe at the gym while you're working out, or volunteering at a soup kitchen or for a local charity. You see, the number Six is a number connected to "service to others," so any type of group you're involved with that helps the community in some way is a great place to meet people. This is the year you can make positive changes in your life and in love.

Number Seven Love Year

This is a legal year. If of age, this year you'll get your driver's license or a job. If you're over eighteen, you could get engaged or even married, but don't be so quick to jump the gun, because the Seven year is the divorce year, too! Of course, maybe none of these things will happen, but if you're heading down one of those roads, these are things to consider. Because the number Seven is a very spiritual number, this year will be filled with "higher thinking" on your part. You want a deep, meaningful relationship. It's also a time when you can easily draw your soul mate. One of your past life connections will cross your path. Are you ready? You may be surprised as to who he or she really is! There will be many love lessons. Some good. Some not so good. You could become obsessed with someone. It seems your love life is big news this year! You'll be the talk of the town or the subject of gossip, so keep your reputation in check!

Number Eight Love Year

Traditionally, the number Eight year brings loads of money, but how does that translate into love? You could date a wealthy guy or some cute girl might drop a bundle on you. Maybe your admirer will shower you with beautiful gifts. On the other hand, be careful that you aren't trying to buy someone's affection. Don't go overboard on dates. It's okay to pay for your own meal every now and then. Someone may try to use you because of your generous heart. Don't be fooled. If you feel that someone is taking advantage of your good nature, call him or her on it. On a positive note, you will likely draw someone to you who is strong and self-assured, and someone who spends his or her money freely. Expect some great dates with no expense spared.

Number Nine Love Year

This year wraps up your entire nine-year cycle. You deal with the karma of the past eight years. In other words, there are love lessons you still need to learn. Anything you didn't do or handle correctly in the previous cycles, you must address now. You have no choice. Some people fear the approaching Nine year, and others are not affected by it at all because they have lived their cycles correctly. Many times the past will come back to haunt you. If you ended a relationship badly with your ex, you'll probably meet up to make amends. However, if you want to get back together with someone you've broken up with, the number Nine love cycle is a time to do just that. It's a time of endings and breakups for many. For some, it's a time to rekindle a relationship or get back together. Let's say you had a major crush on someone and that person didn't even notice you a year ago; this year he or she could be attracted to you! If you want to make amends with a friend, now's the time to go back and rectify the situation. Do it in a number Nine love year because your number One love year starts on your next birthday, and that means only one thing: *new* beginnings and *new* love!

Conclusion

Whenever you affirm the positive in you, you are affirming the positive in your relationships with others. Special friendships and love are easily drawn to you. If you like yourself, others will be attracted to your positive energy. Think of a very popular guy at your school. Everyone seems to like him. Teachers are nice to him. Underclassmen look up to him. Girls love to be seen with this guy. What's he got that others don't? A sense of self-confidence, and that confidence helps him spread his wings. He can go that extra mile and score a winning touchdown, or take an honors math class.

How about that girl who isn't a beauty queen but all the guys think she's cute? She's fun and flirty. Even though she doesn't wear the latest designer clothes and isn't a straight A student, kids still think she's "all that." This "average" girl probably doesn't think she's "average." She knows she's special, and that makes a difference in how people see her. When you feel good about who you are, you will talk, walk, and carry yourself differently than if you're down on yourself.

If you don't have movie star looks and can't dribble a basketball, so what? Everyone is born with different talents. Find out what your talents are and start using them. Expand on them. The best way to build self-confidence is to do something that you are great at. If you have a flair for writing, start a school newspaper. If you love photography, join the yearbook staff and snap tons of pictures around school. Everyone lives to get his or her picture in the yearbook. You'd certainly get a lot of attention with a camera around your neck! All teens feel ugly at times, or stupid, or unlovable—even the most popular kids worry about how they are perceived. They have reputations to uphold! But they don't allow themselves to think negative thoughts for too long. No one wants to be around someone who is always down. It's a drag!

But back to being in love. . . . To fall in love can transform our very being. It can make us a better person. On an unconscious level, we all know this. That's why everyone is seeking and searching for this unique connection. Honor the loving spirit that lies within you and one another.

Begin by looking at all of the relationships that enter your life as a gift. Whether these relationships are a positive or negative influence, each person possesses a gift to help you grow spiritually. Chance meetings are not coincidental. The people you ride next to on the bus or sit close to in class have a purpose in your life—a divine purpose. Who you choose to be with romantically or choose to love is even deeper.

The next time you meet someone, think for a moment, "What am I supposed to learn from this person?" Even if you politely strike up a conversation with someone for a few minutes while waiting in the lunch line, there's something to learn. Maybe someone just flashes you a smile and that brightens your mood.

Each and every one of us is divine. We have a physical sense, but also a spiritual sense. Because we can see, hear, and touch each other physically, it's easy to look at others in only a physical way. But take a moment to ponder a friend's spiritual essence. How do you "feel" about him or her? Most of the time when we reflect back on our friendships and relationships, we understand why a certain person was in our life.

I urge you to begin looking at your relationships in the spiritual sense. And feel blessed. We all come together for a purpose. The most meaningful part of life is not getting an expensive dress or winning a trophy or buying a cool car—

it's our relationships with others. There are constant exchanges each and every day, and they may be more meaningful than you can imagine.

Throughout your life, people will come and go. Some will touch your life more than others. There will be great loves and there will be people who may break your heart. There will be someone you'll never forget and someone you'll never let go of. Love changes our lives. Allowing yourself to be open to the most powerful emotion we possess is truly a gift. Love is the best gift you can give someone and the greatest gift you can receive. Be open to all of your opportunities to create and share love in your life!

LLEWELLYN ORDERING INFORMATION

Order Online:

Visit our website at www.llewellyn.com, select your books, and order them on our secure server.

Order by Phone:

- Call toll-free within the U.S. at 1-877-NEW-WRLD (1-877-639-9753). Call toll-free within Canada at 1-866-NEW-WRLD (1-866-639-9753)
- We accept VISA, MasterCard, and American Express

Order by Mail:

Send the full price of your order (MN residents add 7% sales tax) in U.S. funds, plus postage & handling to:

Llewellyn Worldwide
P.O. Box 64383, Dept. 0-7387-0545-4
St. Paul, MN 55164-0383, U.S.A.

Postage & Handling:

Standard (U.S., Mexico, & Canada). If your order is:
$49.99 and under, add $3.00
$50.00 and over, FREE STANDARD SHIPPING

AK, HI, PR: $15.00 for one book plus $1.00 for each additional book.

International Orders (airmail only):
$16.00 for one book plus $3.00 for each additional book

Orders are processed within 2 business days. Please allow for normal shipping time.
Postage and handling rates subject to change.

Maria Shaw's Star Gazer
Your Soul Searching, Dream Seeking, Make Something Happen Guide to the Future

MARIA SHAW

The only comprehensive guide to the New Age written for teens. You've seen her on Fox News, heard her on America Talk Radio. She's been in the national spotlight appearing on television shows from *Blind Date* to *Soap Talk* to the *Anna Nicole Smith Show* (counseling Anna on her personal relationships).

She's Maria Shaw, author of Llewellyn's new *Alternagyrl™ Calendar,* and now the author of a book about the new age written just for ages twelve to eighteen.

Maria Shaw's Star Gazer helps teens discover who they are through their zodiac signs. It gives a numerology formula to predict the next nine years of life; how-tos for reading palms, the tarot, and auras; guides to crystals, candle magic, and dreams; and techniques for developing intuitive abilities.

0-7387-0422-9
336 pp., 7½ x 9⅛, illus. $17.95

To order, call 1-877-NEW-WRLD
Prices subject to change without notice

Maria Shaw's Tarot Kit for Teens

MARIA SHAW

A fun introduction to the Tarot—exclusively for young adults.

Teens who want to discover and unlock their psychic abilities will find no better guide than Maria Shaw, who has a knack for making new age topics accessible to the young adult market.

Maria covers all the basics, from a smattering of history to in-depth descriptions of all major and minor arcana cards. Common concerns such as how to prepare for a reading, how to cut the cards, how to ask questions, and how to choose the best days for readings are discussed in detail. Sixteen different card spreads, including teen love layouts, the guardian angel/spirit guide spread, and the big question spread, give new readers lots of options.

The deck itself is age-appropriate, containing nonthreatening images that are appealing to young adult interests.

0-7387-0523-3
Boxed kit (5½ x 8⅝)
Includes 78 full-color cards, black bag, and 192 pp. illus. guidebook $19.95

Blue is for Nightmares

LAURIE FARIA STOLARZ

Sixteen-year-old Stacey Brown isn't the most popular girl at her boarding school, or the prettiest, or the smartest. She has confidence issues, a crush on the boyfriend of her best friend Drea, and she has painful secrets. Stacy is also a hereditary Witch. Now she's having nightmares that someone is out to murder Drea.

Guilt plagues Stacey because a series of dreams several years earlier predicted a death she couldn't prevent. Now she is determined to use her skills (including folk magick, dream magick and contacting her grandmother's ghost) to find the killer before the killer finds Drea. Edgy and engaging, Laurie Faria Stolarz takes her readers on an unforgettable ride with this witchy thriller.

0-7387-0391-5
288 pp., 5³⁄₁₆ x 8 $9.95

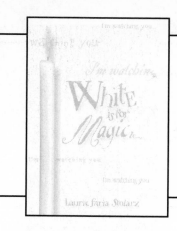

White is for Magic

LAURIE FARIA STOLARZ

Stacey's nightmares are back . . .

It's been a year since Stacey rescued her best friend Drea from being murdered. Now, Stacey is experiencing another series of nightmares that foretell murder, and this time Stacey is the one in danger! To make matters worse, Drea is flirting with Stacey's boyfriend; creepy transfer students are obsessed with last year's murder; and Stacey is receiving threatening notes that prove her premonitions are true.

With help from her mother and her grandmother's spells, Stacey gains the strength and wisdom to face her fears and past demons. But will it be enough to find the killer in time to save her life?

0-7387-0443-1
312 pp., 5³⁄₁₆ x 8

$8.95